D1712987

Internment

JAPANESE AMERICANS
IN WORLD WAR II

PUBLIC PERSECUTIONS   Ruth Bjorklund

Cavendish
Square
New York

Published in 2017 by Cavendish Square Publishing, LLC
243 5th Avenue, Suite 136, New York, NY 10016

Copyright © 2017 by Cavendish Square Publishing, LLC
First Edition

Website: cavendishsq.com

This publication represents the opinions and views of the author based on
his or her personal experience, knowledge, and research. The information
in this book serves as a general guide only. The author and publisher
have used their best efforts in preparing this book and disclaim liability
rising directly or indirectly from the use and application of this book.

CPSIA Compliance Information: Batch #CW17CSQ

All websites were available and accurate when this book was sent to press.

Library of Congress Cataloging-in-Publication Data

Names: Bjorklund, Ruth, author.
Title: Internment : Japanese Americans in World War II / Ruth Bjorklund.
Description: New York : Cavendish Square Publishing, [2017] |
Series: Public persecutions | Includes bibliographical references and index.
Identifiers: LCCN 2016026819 (print) | LCCN 2016031733 (ebook) |
ISBN 9781502623232 (library bound) | ISBN 9781502623249 (ebook)
Subjects: LCSH: Japanese Americans–Evacuation and relocation,
1942-1945–Juvenile literature. |
World War, 1939-1945–Japanese Americans–Juvenile literature.
Classification: LCC D769.8.A6 B574 2017 (print) | LCC D769.8.A6 (ebook) |
DDC 940.53/1773089956–dc23
LC record available at https://lccn.loc.gov/2016026819

Editorial Director: David McNamara
Editor: Fletcher Doyle
Copy Editor: Nathan Heidelberger
Associate Art Director: Amy Greenan
Designer: Stephanie Flecha
Production Coordinator: Karol Szymczuk

The photographs in this book are used by permission and through the courtesy of:
Cover Dorothea Lange/Education Images/UIG/Getty Images; pp. 4, 11 Keystone-France/Gamma-Keystone/
Getty Images; pp. 7, 8, 46, 51, 69, 75, 99 Bettmann/Getty Images; p. 17 North Wind Picture Archives; p.
21 Buyenlarge/Getty Images; p. 24 Museum of History and Industry; p. 27 Bain News Service/Library of
Congress; p. 29 Dave Buresh/The Denver Post/Getty Images; pp. 34, 60 Popperfoto/Getty Images; p. 37
Buyenlarge Archive/UIG/Bridgeman Images; p. 39 ullstein bild/Getty Images; p. 43 Library of Congress;
p. 56 NY Daily News Archive/Getty Images; p. 63 U.S. Army Signal Corps photo/Library of Congress/
Corbis/VCG/Getty Images; p. 72 Clem Albers/Library of Congress; p. 79 Dorothea Lange/Everett
Historical/Shutterstock; p. 88 nsf/Alamy Stock Photo; p. 92 Rondal Partridge/FSA/Library of Congress/
File:Dorothea Lange atop automobile in California.jpg/Wikimedia Commons; p. 97 Harris & Ewing/Library
of Congress; p. 100 AP Images; p. 105 Paul Kitagaki Jr./Sacramento Bee/MCT/Getty Images; p. 109 Mark
Kauffman/The LIFE Images Collection/Getty Images; p. 111 Robyn Beck/AFP/Getty Images; p. 112 Joe
Mabel/File:Bainbridge Island Japanese American Exclusion Memorial 19.jpg/Wikimedia Commons.

Printed in the United States of America

Contents

Rapid Backlash

"They were marked as different from other races and were not treated on an equal basis," wrote humanitarian Eleanor Roosevelt, wife of President Franklin D. Roosevelt. In a 1943 magazine article, she described the racial prejudice and forced evacuation being endured by Japanese Americans during World War II. "In one part of our country they were feared as competitors, and the rest of our country knew them so little and cared so little about them that they did not even think about the principle that we in this country believe in—that of equal rights for all human beings." As the First Lady stated, the Bill of Rights assures equal rights for all, yet in 1941, most people in the country, including her husband, ignored the Constitution and turned their backs on Japanese Americans.

On December 7, 1941, Japanese bombers executed a deadly and unprovoked surprise attack on US naval ships anchored in Pearl Harbor, on the island of Oahu in Hawaii.

Opposite: President Franklin D. Roosevelt addresses Congress and the nation, announcing the Japanese attack on Pearl Harbor.

The next day, President Roosevelt stood before Congress to request a declaration of war. His statements were brief. "America was suddenly and deliberately attacked by naval and air forces of the Empire of Japan ... Hostilities exist. There is no blinking at the fact that our people, our territory, and our interests are in grave danger." His request could barely be heard above the thunderous roar of approving members of Congress.

As Congress declared war on Japan on December 8, 1941, the United States made its entry into World War II. Americans were immediately enveloped in fear. As people girded for war, most regarded Japanese Americans, including those that had become US citizens, as "enemy aliens."

After the attack, the full force of decades of anti-Japanese prejudice exploded. Derogatory remarks and bigoted epithets were used in everyday conversation as well as in public. Newspapers ran headlines denouncing "Japs" or "Nips," a term derived from **Nippon**, the name by which the Japanese people call their country. The airwaves shrieked with dread over the threat of the "Yellow Peril."

When the government issued an **internment** order, resulting in more than 120,000 Japanese Americans being relocated to concentration camps in remote, desolate parts of the American West, few non-Japanese Americans protested. The mass incarceration of American citizens and legal residents based solely upon their Japanese ancestry was rarely deemed unlawful. The United States military never had to prove that the Japanese Americans posed a military threat or that internment would make the nation safer from attack.

From big cities to small towns, anti-Japanese sentiment was rampant throughout the western United States.

By and large, most Japanese Americans peacefully accepted their fate. There were few resistors or protestors, although confusion and uncertainty overwhelmed them. Most Japanese Americans believed that American ideals and values would not be abandoned and held the belief that the alarming situation was temporary. This proved incorrect. On April 30, 1942, Japanese Americans were given a week to gather personal items and dispense with the rest of their belongings. Not until March 1946 were the last of the imprisoned Japanese Americans released from the internment camps.

ONE

The Ancient and the New

Japanese citizens began arriving on American shores in the middle of the nineteenth century. As with other **immigrants**, they left their homeland for numerous reasons and sought the promise of freedom and opportunity the United States offered. Between the 1860s and the early 1920s, more than 350,000 Japanese men and women immigrated to the United States. The Hawaii Territory and the American mainland's Pacific coast received most of the immigrants. The Japanese newcomers were confident and optimistic, and few anticipated the difficult challenges they would encounter.

US-Japanese Relations

For more than 350 years, the Empire of Japan was ruled by the Tokugawa shogunate, a group of military commanders, or **shoguns**. The shoguns served feudal lords, and samurai warriors served the shoguns. The country's emperor was a deeply beloved figurehead who was allowed only to preside

Opposite: Young Japanese picture brides arrive in the United States to marry Japanese men they have never met.

over ceremonies. When a young emperor named Meiji took the throne in 1868, after the shogunate was toppled, he and his advisors set about dispensing with the shoguns and their lords. They got rid of feudalism. Meiji was very interested in American history, culture, and literature. He wanted to modernize Japanese society. He dismantled Japan's social caste system, improved manufacturing output, provided education for girls as well as boys, and created a modern army with advanced weapons and Western-influenced military strategies. His efforts cut a wide swath through society. Many of the upper classes, including samurais and shoguns, were disenfranchised.

During the reign of the Tokugawa shogunate, the Japanese Empire remained isolated from Europe and European colonies, including the United States, Canada, and Latin America. **Emigration** was virtually forbidden. In the middle of the nineteenth century, policies and attitudes began to change. At the forefront of the pressure to change was the Industrial Revolution. Western nations were advancing rapidly in their technology and production while Asia lagged far behind. Western governments wanted to expand the scope of their trade in manufactured goods and looked to Asia for new prospects. Britain chose to force China into trade agreements and went to war twice to seize land and develop trading ports. Other nations, including the United States, thereafter were able to sign trade agreements with China. In the meantime, the Japanese government looked warily at China's military defeat and their forced participation in trade agreements. The Japanese wanted to improve their economy,

Naval Commodore Matthew Perry opened the door to trade with Japan.

but instead of choosing to conduct trade negotiations with foreign governments, the Japanese government turned sharply away. Japan went once again into isolation.

In the meantime, the United States had developed a robust trade with China and other countries in the Pacific—the Philippines, Guam, and the Kingdom of Hawaii. A steady stream of sailing ships laden with goods moved across the Pacific from North America to Asian ports. New merchant ships were invented and built, so no longer did traders need to use slow-moving sailing ships. They had the advantage of operating modern steamships powered by coal. Merchants needed to establish coaling stations along their Pacific routes so they could anchor, refuel, and take on provisions. Japan was in an ideal geographic position to provide these services, and in addition, it was believed that Japan held substantial deposits of coal. The United States decided to approach Japan and firmly request that the government open its ports to US ships.

In 1853, President Millard Fillmore dispatched Commodore Matthew Perry of the US Navy to Tokyo, Japan. Arriving on July 8 of that year, Commodore Perry was accompanied by a squadron of two sailing vessels, a frigate, and two steamships. Japanese bystanders witnessing the arrival of the fleet denounced its coming as "black ships of evil mien." ("Mien" means "appearance.") Japanese officials at first refused to speak to the commodore but relented as they eyed the powerful ships and crews of soldiers. Japan had no navy with which to defend itself, and government officials knew that any refusal would likely lead to a greater show of force. Commodore Perry was ultimately allowed to deliver a letter from President Fillmore and then returned to the United States. He returned a year later with a larger squadron to receive the Japanese government's response. The Japanese were very reluctant to agree to the American president's proposals, but they did so. The two governments signed the Treaty of Kanagawa on March 31, 1854. The treaty contained several provisions that were far more favorable to the United States than to Japan. Commodore Perry's mission opened the doors to future trade and greater interaction with Japan.

After several years of technological and economic advancement, Japan succumbed to a civil war not unlike the American Civil War. During what was called the Boshin War, in 1868 and 1869, shogunate supporters tried to regain power from the emperor. Emperor Meiji read a great deal about Abraham Lincoln, a leader who united a nation despite the bloodshed it caused. In following his example, Meiji was determined to transform his country and beat back the Tokugawa shoganate. In November of 1868, Meiji's restoration army was victorious. Japanese society underwent a major political and social revolution. In 1889, Emperor Meiji issued the nation's first constitution.

Afterward, Japan grew increasingly urban and industrial. The change in society was dramatic. Long a nation of farmers and rural communities, Japan confiscated farmland to encourage the growth of cities and manufacturing. Farmers and villagers were forced out of their homes. Many came to the cities to look for factory jobs but found there were few jobs available for untrained, unskilled workers. The holdings of former shoguns and samurais were also confiscated. Many in the country, having lost their livelihoods, had nowhere to turn. At the same time, however, news spread about the thriving economy in the United States. The Japanese government lifted its restriction on emigration, and so many Japanese—nearly all men—made the painful decision to leave their families and emigrate. The government hoped that the emigrants would send money back to Japan. In time, the remittances, or money sent back, amounted to more than two million yen each year.

Hawaiian Immigration

Nearly all of the initial Japanese emigrants went to Hawaii. There, the men were **conscripted** to work on pineapple or sugarcane plantations owned by large American corporations and wealthy, white landowners. Japanese men joined Native Hawaiian, Chinese, and Filipino laborers in the fields, in the strenuous work clearing land, installing irrigation, planting, weeding, and harvesting. They were paid seventeen dollars a month, with only one day off each week. Shifts were ten to twelve hours long, and on many plantations, field bosses used whips to enforce discipline. The labor contracts required workers to work for three to five years. Many workers who completed their contracts returned to Japan and reported the unsanitary housing conditions, the lack of decent food, and the physical abuse they received at the hands of plantation bosses. The Japanese government was indignant and banned emigration. Not until seventeen years later did Japan lift the ban, thus allowing thousands of Japanese workers to resume immigration to Hawaii. Plantation owners were eager to re-employ Japanese laborers. When importing goods to the islands, plantation managers gave traders shopping lists of items such as tea, rice, mules, and horses, and made special requests for "Japs." Before the end of the century, more than eighty thousand Japanese workers had immigrated to Hawaii, and only about half of them returned to Japan after their commitment ended.

Those that remained established Japanese enclaves and formed labor unions to improve working conditions. Japanese women began immigrating to Hawaii to marry men they did not know. Children born of these marriages, called **Nisei**, or second generation, attended Japanese-language schools as well as American public schools. Their parents instilled traditional Japanese values such as showing respect for elders, while the American schools and media instilled belief in democracy, equality, justice, and freedom. By the 1920s, nearly two hundred thousand people of Japanese ancestry had immigrated to Hawaii and made up nearly 40 percent of Hawaii's population.

Coming to the Mainland

Besides many farmworkers and laborers, Japanese immigrants also included artisans, former samurais, merchants, students, and other educated individuals. The first Japanese immigrants to arrive in North America were samurais who had become political refugees. They arrived in 1869 and formed the first Japanese settlement in North America, called the Wakamatsu Silk and Tea Farm Colony. A Dutchman named John Henry Schnell, who resided in Japan and was married to a Japanese woman, was a shogunate sympathizer. When the shogunate fell, he sought to rescue samurais and other ranking shogunate officials. He set up a refugee colony in California for these disenfranchised farmers and businessmen. Schnell enticed twenty-five people to join his colony. They sailed aboard three ships belonging to the Pacific Mail Steamship Company and arrived in San Francisco on May 27, 1869. From there, the immigrants sailed up the Sacramento River to the town of Placerville in El Dorado County, California, near the mining region of Gold Hill. Schnell had previously made arrangements to purchase 160 acres (65 hectares) of land.

The colonists brought with them traditional Japanese crops—thousands of silkworm cocoons for silk farming as well as fifty thousand mulberry trees, the silkworms' diet. They also brought bamboo roots, tea seeds, grape seedlings, and wax trees used for making paper. More than 140,000 tea plants were established as well as fields of rice, a crop not yet grown in California. The colony prospered at first. In 1870, the farmers won prizes at the San Francisco agricultural fair. But in 1871, the crops failed, and most recognized that the fault lay with the miners who intentionally diverted the streams and poisoned the water.

Japanese nationals immigrating to the American mainland faced daunting challenges. There were no more patrons such as Schnell, nor were there any conscription contracts, so immigrants to the mainland needed to find their own work when they arrived. They were at the mercy of labor contractors and also found themselves competing for jobs with Chinese workers. The Chinese were the first Asian people to immigrate to the United States, beginning in the 1850s. Companies building the transcontinental railroads hired thousands of Chinese immigrants when American railroad workers went on strike for better wages and working conditions. The Chinese workers crossed the strikers' picket lines and accepted the low pay and harsh working conditions. For that, the American workers deeply resented the Chinese and accused them of stealing their jobs. In response to public outcry, the US Congress passed a law called the Chinese Exclusion Act of 1882, which halted all Chinese immigration. Unable to take advantage of Chinese workers willing to work for less money, the railroad companies sought another source for low-cost labor and solicited Japanese immigrants.

Japanese laborers endured harsh conditions building the transcontinental railroads.

Several labor contractors, such as the Oriental Trading Company, recruited Japanese workers to install track for the new transcontinental railroads. The company brought workers to California, Oregon, Washington, Canada, Wyoming, Colorado, and the Great Plains to work on the Great Northern, the Northern Pacific, the Union Pacific, and the Central Pacific lines. The contractors transported laborers to different work sites and negotiated labor agreements. The workers did as ordered, worked grueling long hours, and slept in crowded bunkhouses or boxcars with little or no sanitation. They were fed substandard food. They earned a pittance—just $1.10 a day, of which the contractors took 10 cents from each worker. Animosity toward the Japanese quickly developed. They, too, were the subject of anger at the perceived loss of job opportunities for American citizens. Miller Freeman, a high-ranking naval official in Washington State, declared, "My investigation of the situation … convinced me that the increasing accretions of the Japanese were depriving the young white men of the opportunities that they are legitimately entitled to."

At the same time Japanese nationals were coming to the United States to work for the railroads, many Japanese immigrants living in Hawaii opted to join them. They were able to do so because on June 14, 1900, Hawaii became an official territory of the United States and thereby subject to the laws of the US Constitution. In particular, Japanese workers were most affected by the law prohibiting slavery and indentured servitude. This law made their conscripted labor contracts with the sugar and pineapple plantations illegal. Japanese workers and their families celebrated joyfully, with many choosing to leave the plantations permanently. Thousands returned home to Japan, while thousands more immigrated east to the United States, Canada, and South America. By 1900, there were more than twenty-five thousand Japanese nationals on the US mainland.

A large proportion of Japanese immigrants had been displaced farmers, so after their labor contracts with the railroads ended, many took on farmwork, while others worked in mines and lumber mills. Most settled on the West Coast, from Washington State to California, while some went inland to farm and raise livestock in Canada, Colorado, Montana, Idaho, and the Great Plains. Nearly all of the first immigrants were men.

With a greater degree of freedom than those who had been conscripted in Hawaii, many immigrants opted to remain on the mainland indefinitely. As a result, the practice of arranged marriages with "picture brides" became increasingly popular. In Japan, families matched up their sons and daughters. The marriage would take place in Japan. While brides and their families attended the ceremony, just a photograph of the distant groom was in attendance. When the brides stepped off the ships in the ports of Long Beach, San Francisco, or Seattle, they were able to recognize their husbands only because of the photograph. Many brides were sorely disappointed. A fair number of the men had clearly misrepresented themselves— they were older than they stated on their questionnaire, or poorer, or they did not have the jobs or property they claimed to possess. The women were unable to return to Japan. They had hoped for adventure and success, and most were dismayed with the taste of American food, their dirty and uncomfortable living quarters, and their new husbands. They were lonely for the people they left behind. Most women also worked at hard physical labor next to their husbands in the fields. Still, they honored their marriage vows and accepted their fate. They set to raising children and creating strong, close-knit, and traditional communities. Their arrival radically changed the Japanese way of life in America. Where before most Japanese immigrant communities were composed of a migrant, single, male workforce, they became, with the arrival of the women, permanent, family-oriented societies. The women were responsible for establishing schools, places of worship, community centers, and marketplaces.

Japanese Communities

As railroad and mining contracts ended, many Japanese immigrants began working in agriculture and fishing, both traditional occupations in Japan. By the 1920s, a large proportion of Japanese workers gave up their migrant ways and settled into farming communities in California's Central Valley and Central Coast; the fertile valleys of Central Oregon; the Oregon coast; and the Yakima Valley, the shores of Lake Washington, and Bainbridge Island in Washington State. When major irrigation projects were completed to supply water to dry regions of Idaho and Utah, more jobs for Japanese workers opened up on sugar beet farms in those areas. Japanese farmworkers also settled in Colorado, Montana, the Great Plains, and British Columbia, Canada. Most worked in the sugar beet industry, while others raised livestock or worked in meat-packing operations.

The Japanese have traditionally regarded farming as an honorable occupation, with its ability to "feed the nation." In Japan, farmers ranked socially just beneath the samurais. After leaving the hard labor of railroad construction and mining, the **Issei**, the name for first-generation Japanese immigrants, worked for American farmers until they could save enough to buy or lease land. Many took over land unwanted by American farmers, and with their traditional techniques of efficient irrigation and cultivation, they produced abundant crops.

A California state investigation in 1909 reported that Japanese farmers posted impressive statistics regarding yield, efficient use of small parcels of land, and variety and quality

The success of Japanese immigrant farmers angered American agriculture groups, resulting in a rash of restrictive land laws.

of their crops. The report concluded that the Issei farmers could have taught Americans better farming methods, had American farmers not been so unwilling to communicate. But anti-Japanese prejudice was increasing. The Issei believed independence was the best route to a good and honorable life. They were exceptionally frugal, forgoing personal comforts for the hard work needed to attain the goal of self-sufficiency and financial success.

The Asiatic Exclusion League (AEL), initially called the Japanese and Korean Exclusion League, was founded in San Francisco 1905 to oppose Japanese immigration and to send Japanese immigrants back to Japan. The AEL referred to the efforts of the Issei farmers as "taking up California lands." Newspapers decried the Issei farmers' thriftiness and called them "unhygienic shack-dwellers." At this point, the anti-Japanese movement did not have legal backing that would allow them to discriminate officially against Asian farmworkers trying to achieve financial success. The anti-Chinese discrimination spilled over into malicious and vindictive racial discrimination against Japanese immigrants. Discrimination was displayed in many overt ways, such as the unwillingness of Americans to sell land to the Issei outright or the practice of taking over Issei farms after they had been improved and developed. Issei farmers raised and sold their crops of rice, hops, strawberries, melons, celery, sugar beets, and Muscat grapes used to make raisins. They were most successful planting and harvesting grapes and strawberries because most American farmers did not relish the painstaking labor involved. In a book titled *The American Japanese Problem*, the author Sidney Gulick wrote, "[Strawberry farming] illustrates the stooping work for which Japanese farmers are particularly adapted." Some Japanese farmers living close to cities used their traditional and refined horticultural skills to establish nurseries for urban and suburban gardens. Regardless of the challenges and prejudice, many Japanese farmers were very successful. In California by 1920, for example, Issei farmers cultivated more than 450,000 acres (182,100 ha) of farmland.

Along the coastlines of California, Oregon, Washington, and Alaska, many Japanese immigrants entered the fishing industry. They worked on boats and in canneries. Many sold fresh fish off the fishermen's wharves. In 1888, an influential labor newsletter, *Coast Seaman's Journal*, warned about the "recently developed phase of the Mongolian issue." ("Mongolian" at the time was used as a derogatory reference to people with physical features such as high cheekbones and a fold of skin in the upper eyelid.) The newspaper the *Morning Call* declared that the Japanese were "taking work away from our boys and girls and men and women." However, by the late 1920s, there were eight Japanese-owned fishing companies in Monterrey, California, alone, and several dozen more could be found up and down the West Coast. Fishers, too, developed tightly knit communities along the Pacific coast.

Successful farming and fishing enterprises fostered rapid growth of Japanese communities. Originally, most immigrants had planned to return to Japan, but as more and more people began having children, families decided to stay in their adopted country. Japanese communities continued to grow when many immigrants wrote back to friends and relatives and urged them to come to America.

Urban Living

Not all Japanese immigrants settled in rural areas and became farmers or fishers. Many opted instead to remain in cities. Most settled in San Francisco, the main receiving port for Asian immigrants. Many of these educated immigrants had been merchants, artisans, samurais, bankers, lawyers, and other professional occupations. In San Francisco, they formed a large commercial district known as "Japantown." However, in 1906, an earthquake struck San Francisco, and a subsequent fire burned several neighborhoods, including most of the Japanese neighborhood. It was thereafter that many Japanese city dwellers moved on to other cities, such as Seattle and Los Angeles. Many of the Japanese newcomers to Seattle moved next to the already existing "Chinatown" south of the city. In Los Angeles, they formed a large Japanese community, known as "Little Tokyo."

Most of the Issei who sought work in manufacturing and craftsmen's trades such as carpentry or construction were shut out of trade unions. The Issei had no choice but to work in agriculture or operate businesses. The Issei who had run businesses in Japan saw the opportunity to establish businesses within the developing Japanese communities. They established business districts, either in the small Japantowns

Seattle's Japantown had a thriving business community in the 1940s before the residents were sent to internment camps.

"School Boys"

In the later part of the nineteenth century, many young Japanese men left Japan to obtain an education in the United States. They often came from the upper classes, those families affiliated with the former shogunate. The more well-to-do attended Ivy League universities on the East Coast, but most attended universities in San Francisco, Seattle, and Portland. They were known as "school boys" and received room and board from white families in exchange for domestic services.

within farming and fishing towns or in larger cities such as San Francisco; Los Angeles; Portland, Oregon; and Seattle. The entrepreneurs purveyed goods and services to other Japanese community members. They opened general stores, restaurants, tailor shops, laundries, employment services, and small hotels and boarding houses. In larger cities, the more successful Issei entrepreneurs owned large grocery and department stores and tailoring chains that served the general public.

The Issei formed business and cultural organizations such as the Japanese American Association, the Japan Society, and the Japanese American Citizens League. The organizations, which continue to this day, provided language learning assistance, financial support and advice, business and legal support, housing and employment services, and educational and cultural programming. The organizations also acted on behalf of the Japanese in their social, political, and economic interactions with non-Japanese citizens.

Trials of Assimilation

Most US residents did not accept the Japanese immigrants into the larger American society. The Japanese were often associated with the Chinese and other Asian populations that were resented before the Japanese arrived. Japanese culture seemed too foreign to belong in America. The Japanese created a community. They built Buddhist temples and Christian churches and practiced **Shinto**, an ancient, singularly Japanese religion. They built community centers which served as Japanese language schools for their children as well as places to learn about Japanese culture. Their theaters offered traditional entertainment—Noh theater, Taiko drumming, films, martial arts lessons, poetry readings, and potlucks—and their holidays, ceremonies, weddings, and parties were celebrated in traditional ways. They also built bathhouses, sumo wrestling rings, and baseball diamonds. Successful Japantowns also featured restaurants serving Japanese foods, such as sushi and noodle dishes; bars; billiard rooms; and shops selling Japanese groceries and herbal medicines. Artists and artisans who sold their wares included potters, painters, calligraphers, and furniture makers.

Within their communities, the Japanese followed customs such as removing shoes before entering a house and dining at a low table while seated or kneeling on the floor. The Japanese celebrated traditional holidays such as Girls' Day on March 3, where girls displayed their dolls throughout their home, and Boys' Day on May 5, where carp, a fish that symbolizes happiness and strength, is prepared in a special dish. The boys are often given a gift of a kite, decorated with images of carp. On New Year's Day, Japanese families celebrated by eating distinctive Japanese foods, such as rice cakes, herring eggs, and a roasted carp splayed out and contorted to make the fish appear to be swimming. Additionally, on New Year's Day, people paid all their debts, exchanged greeting cards, and toasted one another with a fermented rice drink called sake. Dessert was mochi, a sweet, gooey rice ball, garnished with tangerines. With these outward displays of Japanese culture, the Japanese were seen by Americans as "alien." The Issei, feeling ostracized, kept close ties to Japan and Japanese ways and culture.

A Nisei man wears traditional Japanese clothing during a celebration on New Year's Day.

A Family's Story

In 1902, sixteen-year old Masuo Yasui immigrated to the United States. He signed up with a Seattle labor contractor who sent him to work on a railroad gang in Montana. As soon as he could, he left and moved to Hood River, Oregon, a small town along the Columbia River. There were hundreds of Japanese Americans working in the area, in sawmills, logging camps, and fruit orchards. Yasui wrote his brother in Japan, urging him to come and help set up a store. In 1912, Yasui married a former girlfriend from Japan, Shidzuyo Miyake, a teacher. They bought farmland, planted orchards, and successfully ran their Hood River store, which acted as an unofficial Japanese community center.

When the United States declared war on Japan, Yasui, a visible Japanese community leader, was immediately arrested and imprisoned. His daughter, Michi, a class salutatorian at the University of Oregon, was slated to speak at her graduation ceremony, but she was denied the right to graduate with her class because attending would put her in violation of the 8:00 p.m. curfew imposed on Japanese Americans. Michi's brother, Min, was the first Japanese American to graduate from the University of Oregon Law School. When his father was arrested, he quit his job and offered to join the army, but was denied. Min protested the curfew and was arrested and put in solitary confinement. He lost his citizenship, was disbarred from practicing law, and eventually was sent with the rest of his family to the Tule Lake Internment Camp in California.

Michi Yasui finally received her diploma from the University of Oregon in 1988.

The Ancient and the New   29

After attending schools in America, the Nisei, or second-generation Japanese youths, were torn between the modern American culture and the traditional culture of Japan. Issei parents encouraged their children to learn the customs and cultures of both societies—in art, music, fashion, manners, and popular culture. Many Nisei had a difficult time blending the two cultures. Some found themselves adopting one over the other. In many communities, Americans were very vocal about their refusal to accept any portion of Asian culture. In Arizona, the Anti-Alien Association threatened to pillage Japanese homes and told residents to "get out or be put out." Many Nisei abandoned the culture of their heritage and sought to become completely "Americanized."

No matter what their social and economic class had been in Japan, in the United States the Japanese relied on the code of conduct of the upper-class samurais to guide and strengthen them. The code, called **Bushido**, included such attributes as courage and determination, unwavering loyalty to their own people and to Japan, a formal and ritualistic politeness, courtesy towards those regarded as "inferiors," and respect for elders. Children were taught to never do anything that might bring shame or disgrace to the family or community, as well as to never cause others to laugh at them. Bushido also required that people not display any emotion. In any confrontation or difficult circumstance, the Issei controlled their tempers and their facial expressions. Americans often interpreted the Japanese aloof demeanor negatively—calling the Japanese "inscrutable," which means impossible to understand or mysterious. The Issei suffered in many ways. Confronted often with racial prejudice as well as restrictions, such as being unable to purchase land or property, the Issei were still determined to succeed and advance in American society. They encouraged their children, the Nisei, to achieve what had been mostly denied to the Issei. With loving pressure from their parents, a large population of Nisei children studied hard, excelled in college, and successfully pursued professional careers, thus bringing honor to their families and community. When the children of the Nisei displayed such academic competence and success, envy and discrimination by whites escalated.

Despite their many accomplishments in construction, farming, fishing, mining, and business, the Japanese, much like the Chinese, faced mounting resentment. For example, the San Francisco school board in 1907 acquiesced to residents' demands and ordered Japanese students and some Korean students to be transferred to the Oriental Public School, a segregated Chinese school. The Japanese were often discriminated against in housing and employment. The San Francisco earthquake and fire left thousands of residents homeless. When new housing tracts were built, bankers, property owners, and real estate agents colluded and ran newspaper advertisements assuring potential homebuyers that there would be no bars, cheap apartments, or Japanese allowed. While most interactions between the Japanese and whites were constrained and couched in distrust, they were generally, but not always, nonviolent.

The AEL was a white supremacist group founded originally under the name Japanese and Korean Exclusion League. It felt the United States should belong only to English-speaking people of European descent. Members of the AEL included top labor union leaders and a future mayor of San Francisco, and the group's influence not only affected California legislators but also members of Congress in Washington, DC. *Organized Labor* was published by a member of the AEL. A story published in it in 1906 contains statements such as, "As long as California is white man's country, it will remain one of the grandest and best states in the union, but the moment the Golden State is subjected to an unlimited Asiatic coolie invasion there will be no more California." The article continued, "The literature and statistics sent out by the Japanese and Korean Exclusion League has done wonderful work in educating the public. Thousands of fair-minded and well-meaning people who were biased and ignorant on the question of Japanese immigration have during the last year, entirely changed their views on the subject."

Newspapers, journals, and other media weighed in on the anti-Japanese question. While some tempered their articles and editorials, others, such as the *Sacramento Bee* and the *Seattle Star,* went a long way in promoting racist propaganda. The *Seattle Star* ran inflammatory headlines such as "Jap Stole White Wife's Love" or "One-Third of Our Hotels Jap Owned." The newspaper also was quick to run any stories about anti-Japanese protests. V. S. McClatchy, publisher of the *Sacramento Bee*, vehemently spoke out against the Japanese. He financed several anti-Japanese pamphlets and was a founder of the Japanese Exclusion League of California. Beginning in 1905, the *San Francisco*

Chronicle ran a campaign against Japanese immigrants, publishing such remarks as, "The little brown men pose a grave peril to California."

The AEL and similar organizations took footholds up and down the West Coast. In 1907, a racist riot broke out in the northern city of Bellingham, Washington, and stirred up anti-Asian immigration proponents there. Many Asians fled across the border into Vancouver, British Columbia, and with them came anti-Asian furor. A rally in Vancouver attracted thousands of anti-immigration demonstrators who broke into violence and vandalism throughout Asian neighborhoods, including Vancouver's Japantown. Rioters demanded a "White Canada." Likewise, in several railroad towns in Idaho, where former Japanese railroad employees had settled, gangs of white rioters joined forces to drive the Japanese families out.

In Seattle, Washington, the Anti-Japanese League was comprised of members of the American Legion, Veterans of Foreign Wars, and Washington State's Veteran's Welfare Commission, and was led by a Washington state legislator. In Oregon, former governor and congressman Walter Pierce was blatant about his anti-Japanese position. His speeches were full of incendiary remarks, such as, "We are white and Christian. They are yellow and do not accept Christianity. We believe in democracy and individualism. They are totalitarian and believe in the divinity of their emperor. Japanese are aggressive and ever plotting for racial supremacy … There is room in the world for both of us, but not on this continent."

TWO

The Squall Before the Storm

Japan's emergence as a formidable foe in World War II had its origins in the Meiji Restoration. It was then, in 1868, when Japan first developed a thirst for wealth, military power, and international respect. The Japanese government resented the treaties they had been forced to sign with Western nations and also bore the weight that population growth was having on Japan's natural resources. Japan, in its pursuit of modern power, needed oil, coal, and steel to industrialize. It began a policy of expansion into other countries and territories to gain access to their natural resources.

By 1875, Japan was making major strides in developing Western technology and with its newfound power, forced Korea to open itself to foreign trade. Japan insisted that Korea, which was then controlled by China, declare itself independent. Tensions arose between China and Japan, but they signed a treaty agreeing to a Chinese withdrawal

Opposite: In 1905, the Japanese army surprised the world with its defeat of Russia in the Russo-Japanese War.

of troops from Korea. However, their armies continued to provoke one another. The Chinese assassinated the pro-Japanese Korean king, and in retaliation, Japan sank a British warship carrying Chinese troops. War was declared in 1894.

Japan, despite having the smaller army, was more modernized and quickly defeated the Chinese. Japan was encouraged that it was able to establish a foothold into territories beyond its borders. Soon afterward, Germany, France, and Russia demanded that Japan withdraw its troops from Korea. Humiliated, Japan's military pushed forward, and in 1904, Japan entered into a war with Russia (which was aided by German troops) over land claims in Korea and Manchuria. Again, a Japanese victory surprised the rest of the world, and many countries began to regard Japan as Asia's greatest leader. It was the first time that an Asian power had defeated a European power. Heady with accomplishment, Japan's military advised the government to pursue an expansionist policy. It was called the "Greater East Asia Co-Prosperity Sphere," and its purpose was to take over regions in Southeast Asia, the Pacific islands, China, Korea, and Taiwan. The generals assured the government that expansion would reap an abundance of natural resources and the raw materials needed to continue modernizing.

World War I

As turmoil around the world churned before the breakout of World War I, Japan was faced with a difficult decision. The Japanese military wanted to retain its Asian possessions and knew that entering the war was likely. Germany was after

The Japanese military reluctantly aligned with Britain and its allies to defend China during World War I.

British holdings in China. But Japan's generals adhered to a policy of "Asia for Asians" and chose to defend China. Furthermore, Japan disliked the Germans for assisting Russia in the Russo-Japanese War and also resented the German leader, Kaiser Wilhelm, who warned the world about the "Yellow Peril" emerging from the Empire of Japan. Japan signed a treaty with Great Britain, China's ally and protector. With an army of more than one million troops and a sizeable fleet, Japan's navy patrolled much of the South Pacific as well as the Pacific coasts of North and South America. The Japanese navy also came to the aid of the Allies by transporting military supplies to forces fighting in the Atlantic. In 1914, Japan officially declared war on Germany and soon after occupied Germany's ports in China and its South Sea territories.

Victory and a Snub

To close out the war and determine the winners' spoils, delegations from the Allies convened for the Versailles Peace Conference. Japan was present and was given a seat in the League of Nations. As a payment for aligning with the victorious Allies, the League of Nations awarded Japan Germany's colonial territories in Micronesia. Japan had become a major international power and the country was honored to be so recognized. However, Japan suffered a serious affront to its dignity, and the result proved to have enormous ramifications just a few decades later. In drafting the Covenant of the League of Nations, the delegation from Japan requested this clause be included in the document:

> The equality of nations being a basic principle of the League of Nations, the High Contracting Parties agree to accord as soon as possible to all alien nationals of states, members of the League, equal and just treatment in every respect making no distinction, either in law or in fact, on account of their race or nationality.

A majority of votes was cast in favor of including the "racial equality" clause. Yet President Woodrow Wilson, the chairman, overturned it, saying that because it was such an important issue, it needed unanimous approval. His veto stemmed from a desire to appease Britain, which had laws giving them the right to colonize non-white peoples, and to appease the racially segregated Southern states of the United States. The leader of the Japanese delegation declared, "We are not too proud to fight but we are too proud to accept a place of admitted inferiority in dealing with one or more of the associated nations. We want nothing but simple justice."

The Japanese media reported on the conference, and when the rejection of the proposal was made clear, negative public opinion toward the United States intensified. It was a turning point for Japan, leading to less cooperation with Western nations and a strengthening of nationalist policies.

Between Wars

In the years after the war, economic depression descended on countries around the world. Many of Japan's Western trading partners put barriers up against trade with Japan in order to protect their markets and the markets of their colonies and territories. Japan continued to pressure China and other parts of Asia. When the League of Nations stood behind China, delegates from Japan walked out on the meeting, protesting that the Western powers were racially motivated to protect their colonies and deny others from assuming their own. By walking out, Japan isolated itself politically from Western nations.

On September 27, 1940, Japan signed the Tripartite Act with Germany and Italy.

By 1940, the German army had overrun Poland, Belgium, the Netherlands, and France, and was targeting the rest of Europe. Japan's military rulers feared that Germany would take control of Europe's Asian colonies—French Indochina and the Netherlands East Indies. These areas were crucial to Japan's supply routes to and from China. Japan's foreign minister pressed his government to align with the Axis Powers—Germany and Italy. Although Japan distrusted Germany's leader, Adolf Hitler, the government nonetheless signed the Tripartite Pact in Berlin, agreeing that Germany, Italy, and Japan would provide mutual assistance should any nation not already at war attack the signatories. The Tripartite Pact, signed in September 1940, acknowledged that Germany and Italy were the new order in Europe and that, in turn, Japan was in control of "Greater East Asia." The pact was a thinly veiled threat to the United States.

Japan continued to look for other sources of raw materials, oil, and gas. It felt threatened on all sides by the United States, Britain, China, and the Netherlands, each of which controlled nearby territory. Japan was afraid that the United States would cut off its oil supply. In 1941, General Hideki Tojo came to power, and with his rise, the Japanese military could now veto any cabinet decision, setting the stage for further confrontation.

Awakening the Sleeping Giant

Japan's annexation of Asian territories, in particular China, was the root cause of the United States, the "sleeping giant," entering World War II. The United States and Japan had long clashed over Japan's occupation of China, and no diplomatic decision between them could be reached. On November 26, 1941, US secretary of state Cordell Hull demanded that Japan withdraw completely from China and Indochina. An embargo was placed on trade with Japan, and its government began to believe that there would be no further negotiations. Japan decided to act quickly and began plotting the "unthinkable." The United States had not yet concluded that a compromise could not be reached.

From that fateful impasse, Japan's military leaders set in motion a bold plan. In a highly calculated and coordinated surprise attack that started just minutes before 8:00 a.m. on December 7, 1941, hundreds of Japanese fighter planes and bombers struck the American naval base at Pearl Harbor on the island of Oahu, Hawaii. The assault lasted just two hours, but it caused utter devastation. The US aircraft carriers and their fighter jets were out to sea and were not able to defend the American fleet. All told, the Japanese military damaged or destroyed twenty vessels, including eight battleships. Nearly two thousand soldiers were killed and more than one thousand were wounded. It was by far the largest and most horrific attack in United States history. On December 8, 1941, President Franklin Roosevelt stood before Congress and made a stirring, six-minute speech, declaring:

> Yesterday, December 7th, 1941—a date which will live in infamy—the United States of America was suddenly and deliberately attacked by naval and air forces of the Empire of Japan. The United States was

at peace with that nation, and, at the solicitation of Japan, was still in conversation with its government and its Emperor looking toward the maintenance of peace in the Pacific. Indeed, one hour after Japanese air squadrons had commenced bombing in the American island of Oahu, the Japanese Ambassador to the United States and his colleague delivered to our Secretary of State a formal reply to a recent American message. And, while this reply stated that it seemed useless to continue the existing diplomatic negotiations, it contained no threat or hint of war or of armed attack. It will be recorded that the distance of Hawaii from Japan makes it obvious that the attack was deliberately planned many days or even weeks ago. During the intervening time the Japanese Government has deliberately sought to deceive the United States by false statements and expressions of hope for continued peace. The attack yesterday on the Hawaiian Islands has caused severe damage to American naval and military forces.

President Roosevelt went on to outline reports of other military moves made by the Japanese, and he concluded his speech by saying:

Hostilities exist. There is no blinking at the fact that our people, our territory and our interests are in grave danger. With confidence in our armed forces, with the unbounding determination of our people, we will gain the inevitable triumph. So help us God. I ask that

Many Americans were against fighting another major war in Europe. Not until the Pearl Harbor bombing did the United States enter World War II.

the Congress declare that since the unprovoked and dastardly attack by Japan on Sunday, December 7th, 1941, a state of war has existed between the United States and the Japanese Empire.

Responding to the president with resounding cheers, Congress declared war on Japan. The next day, Congress declared war on Japan's allies, Italy and Germany. The United States had spent years following a policy of isolationism and two years refusing to enter the war in Europe before Japan "awakened the sleeping giant."

On American Soil

From the very beginning, Japanese immigrants and US citizens generally regarded one another with rancor— socially, culturally, politically, and racially. As the Japanese began immigrating in the late nineteenth century, they were grouped together in the eyes of the Americans with Chinese immigrants, who were earlier arrivals. By the time the first Japanese immigrants set foot on American soil, the Chinese immigrants were already the target of blatant and cruel discrimination in the law, social settings, housing, and in labor markets. The antagonism toward the Chinese spilled over to include the Japanese. Most of the new immigrants were laborers, and as such were dismissed as "coolies."

In many cases, politicians and the media fueled animosity toward Asian newcomers. This resulted in discriminatory laws being passed. At the top of the order were labor issues. United States citizens deeply resented Asians taking jobs they felt should have gone to them. Also, they held a strong prejudice against Asians as a race and were deeply suspicious of Asian culture. Furthermore, most immigrants were single males working in bleak, crowded, and unsanitary conditions. This made it easy for Americans to cast Asians as slovenly, sinful, and unclean.

Some of the laws adversely affecting Asian immigrants were passed as early as 1790. The United States Naturalization Law of March 26, 1790, outlined the rules by which the United States granted national citizenship. Naturalization under the law was limited to immigrants who were "free white persons of good character." It excluded Native Americans, slaves and free blacks, indentured servants, and Asians. After the Civil War, the law was amended to allow "aliens of African nativity and African descent." Asians were still denied the opportunity to become naturalized citizens, and without that ability, they were unable to become US citizens and thus were unable to vote. They were "aliens ineligible for citizenship."

In 1875, a federal immigration law called the Page Act strengthened the ban against "coolie" laborers by making it illegal for a person to come to the United States with a contract to work, thus stemming the immigration of Asian workers. In 1882, the US Congress passed the Chinese Exclusion Act, which halted all Chinese immigration. As a result, more Japanese workers were hired to replace the cheap labor that had been provided by Chinese workers. As the Japanese population in the United States started to rise, many Americans transferred their fear and bigotry toward the Chinese onto the Japanese.

Japanese and Chinese immigrant women await processing in San Francisco.

At the turn of the twentieth century, most Japanese immigrants settled in California, prompting local and regional outrage and demands for a restriction on Japanese immigration, similar to the Chinese Exclusion Act. San Francisco mayor James Phelan echoed the anti-Japanese sentiments of his constituents, declaring, "The Chinese and Japanese are not bona fide citizens. They are not the stuff of which American citizens can be made." In 1900, the *San Francisco Chronicle* began a series of hate-filled articles about the Japanese, further contributing to negative public opinion. The uproar was felt back in Japan, and the Japanese government denied passports for those citizens wishing to emigrate to the United States. However, immigrants were still allowed to enter Canada, Mexico, and South America.

Groups pressured the California legislature to pass anti-Japanese laws. While no laws were immediately passed, in early 1901, on a recommendation from the governor, the legislature adopted a resolution urging the federal government to protect American workers by banning Japanese immigration. In March 1905, the California legislature adopted a resolution demanding that Congress limit the immigration of Japanese workers.

President Theodore Roosevelt agreed in spirit but not with the language of the California resolutions. In a letter dated May 6, 1905, he wrote:

> The California Legislature has the right to protest against the immigration of Japanese laborers. Their cheapness and clannishness make them a challenge to our laboring class, and you may not know that they have begun to present a serious problem in Hawaii—all the more serious because they keep entirely to themselves. Furthermore, I understand that the Japanese themselves do not permit any foreigners to own land in Japan. I would not have objected at all to the California Legislature passing a resolution, courteous and proper in its terms, which would really have achieved their goal. But I do object to, and feel humiliated by, the foolish offensiveness of the resolution they passed.

Californians persisted in their demands to limit the presence of the Japanese. San Francisco was at the forefront of Asian discrimination movements. Not only was the Asiatic

Exclusion League established in the city on May 7, 1905, but the city's outspoken mayor was an avowed racist, although he protested that "the Japanese question with us is not today a race question, but a labor question." He went on to say, "As soon as Japanese coolies are kept out of the country, there will be no danger of irritating these sensitive and aggressive people. They must be excluded because they are non-assimilable; they are a permanently foreign element; they do not bring up families; they do not support churches, schools, nor theaters; in time of trial they will not fight for Uncle Sam, but betray him to the enemy."

Anti-Japanese sentiment was growing rapidly. The AEL led bitter campaigns to oust the newcomers. In an interview in the Boston Herald, Mayor Phelan fueled the bitterness, saying, "California is white man's country, and the two races cannot live side by side in peace, and inasmuch as we discovered the country first and occupied it, we propose to hold it against either a peaceful or a warlike invasion." With this support, the Asiatic Exclusion League focused on halting immigration and segregating the races.

The Gentlemen's Agreement

In 1906, pressure from anti-Japanese citizen groups urged the San Francisco school board to move all Japanese and Korean children into a segregated, Chinese-only school. Supported by the media, the activists called the Japanese students a "morally corrupting influence" on white students. The school board order infuriated the Japanese government to the degree that some officials proposed war.

Japan's victory over Russia in 1905 had established Japan as a serious military rival. President Theodore Roosevelt worried that the fragile relationship the United States maintained with Japan was at risk of falling apart. He sent his secretary of commerce and labor, a Bay-area native, to San Francisco to convince the school board to retract its order. The secretary discovered that only a small portion of the Japanese student population was actually affected. Still, he recommended that the Japanese students should receive "the fullest protection" from the US government. The incident, however, remained of international importance. In his message to Congress in December 1906, the president said, "It's absurd that the mob of a single city may at any time perform acts of lawless violence that would plunge us into war. A city should not be allowed to commit a crime against a friendly nation."

Eventually, President Roosevelt and the Japanese government came to terms over the issue. The president assured the government that no segregation would occur in the public schools. The Japanese, in turn, promised to limit passports to Japanese laborers. The president suggested, although never acted upon, allowing Issei to become citizens. He also agreed that any Japanese citizen who had returned to Japan after residing in the United States could re-enter the country and further agreed that immediate family members of a Japanese citizen working in the United States would be allowed to immigrate. This arrangement became known as "The Gentlemen's Agreement." President Roosevelt summarized the agreement in a letter sent to the secretary of commerce and labor:

My Dear Secretary Metcalf:

I had a talk with the Japanese Ambassador and told him that in my judgment the only way to prevent constant friction between the United States and Japan was to keep the movement of the citizens of each country into the other as restricted as possible to students, travelers, business men and the like. It was necessary that no Japanese laboring men—that is, of the coolie class—come into the United States.

The Ambassador agreed with this view and said that he had always been against Japanese coolies going to America or Hawaii. Of course, San Francisco's action will make it difficult for most Japanese to agree with this view. But I hope my message will smooth over their feelings.

Sincerely yours, Theodore Roosevelt

The Other Washington

Washington State, like California, had many citizens extremely opposed to Japanese immigration. There were thousands of anti-Japanese proponents. Some were active in the Anti-Japanese League, and others were activist citizens fueled by media propaganda. Albert Johnson, initially a newspaper editor, became one of the most influential congressional leaders in the country. He served for twenty years and was instrumental in the passage of the landmark 1924 Immigration Act, otherwise known as the Johnson-Reed Act. While an editor at the *Tacoma News* and the *Grays Harbor Washingtonian*, he was known for his scathing columns against immigrants. He spent eleven years before being elected to Congress "studying" the Japanese and concluded that the country should "put up the bars." Another Seattle newspaper columnist, George N. Mills, published an essay titled "The Japanese Invasion and 'Shinto, the Way of the Gods'" on May 19, 1920. In the article, Mills wrote, "I cannot impress more emphatically on the mind of the American reader the certain disastrous consequences of future Oriental immigration, and why our present policies

This 1920 racist display in Hollywood was not an uncommon sight in the West.

as regards certain Asiatics should be forever abandoned." He goes on to say, "The Shinto religion and government in Japan have been one and the same in the past as well as the present." He charged that anyone of Japanese heritage practicing the Shinto religion would be loyal only to the government of Japan.

Seattle practiced many exclusionary policies, both in the private sector and in government. In 1915, a law was passed barring any Asian immigrants from taking "for sale or profit any salmon or other food or shellfish." Deeds belonging to property owners in many of Seattle's neighborhoods contained discriminatory language, such as, "No person or persons of Asiatic, African or Negro blood, lineage, or extraction shall be permitted to occupy a portion of said property." The *Seattle Star* newspaper ran incendiary headlines such as, "EXCLUSION! The Solution That Means Peace."

Too Good for Their Own Good

Issei workers were barred from factory and office jobs. To make a living, many Issei started their own businesses, such as hotels and restaurants, mainly to serve each other. Many also became fruit and vegetable farmers. They were exceptional farmers and sold their products to wholesalers and the general public. Mayor Phelan lashed out against Japanese farmers in California, saying, "They now occupy valleys in California by lease or purchase of land to the exclusion of not only whites but Chinese, and if this silent invasion is permitted by the federal government, they would at the rate at which they are coming, a thousand a month, soon convert the fairest state in the union into a Japanese colony. If they were naturalized they would outvote us." The mayor and his followers chose to believe they were being threatened. However, those Japanese operating their own farms and businesses were making their own work and not taking jobs away from white Americans. Regardless, resentment remained strong and California agriculture groups pursued strict land limitation laws.

Unions emphatically refused membership to the Japanese. As a result, the Japanese formed their own coalitions, such as the Japanese Association of America and the Japanese Produce Association. They were well organized and able to provide members of their community with capital, labor, and legal support. In 1903, in Oxnard, California, Mexican and Japanese farmworkers joined together to protest a wage cut. They requested that their union become a part of the American Federation of Labor (AFL). The president of the AFL, Samuel Gompers, agreed, as long as there were no Japanese union members. In response, the Mexican leaders wrote:

> In the past we have counseled, fought, and lived on very short rations with our Japanese brothers, and toiled with them in the fields, and they have been uniformly kind and considerate. We would be false to them and to ourselves and to the cause of Unionism if we, now, accepted privileges for ourselves which are not accorded to them … We therefore respectfully petition the A. F. of L. to grant us a charter under which we can unite all the Sugar Beet and Field Laborers of Oxnard, without regard to their color or race. We will

refuse any other kind of charter, except one which will wipe out race prejudices and recognize our fellow workers as being as good as ourselves.

Their request was denied, and the Mexican union members withdrew their application.

In 1919, in Hawaii, the Filipino Labor Union and the Federation of Japanese Labor joined forces to strike for better wages. On December 4, 1919, the unions brought their demands to the Hawaiian Sugar Planters' Association. They wanted pay increased from 77 cents for a ten-hour day to $1.25 for males, and from 58 cents to 95 cents per day and paid maternity leave for females. These requests were far below rates being paid to laborers on the mainland. On July 1, 1920, a compromise was finally reached and the workers were given a 50 percent pay raise and more benefits.

Alien Land Laws

In 1889, Washington State included in its constitution a law disallowing any alien from owning land if the person was ineligible for citizenship, as defined by the Immigration Acts of 1790 and 1875. It was the first Western state to adopt the prohibition of land ownership to Asians and other "ineligible" persons. In 1913, under pressure from anti-immigrant groups and citizens who resented the success of Japanese farmers, California passed an Alien Land Law which prohibited aliens who were not eligible for citizenship—in other words, Asians—from owning land or purchasing long-term leases. Some Japanese went into secret partnership with sympathetic citizens and were able to circumvent the law. Additionally, some Issei farmers put titles to land in their American-born children's names. In the decade after the California law was passed, other state legislatures followed suit. In 1917, Arizona passed a similar law, and subsequently, so did Louisiana, Oregon, Idaho, Montana, and Kansas. Although Washington State already had a similar law on its books, after California's law, it amended its law to deny Issei farmers from putting their land in their children's names.

Citizenship Denied

In 1922, Congress passed the Cable Act, which overturned a law that revoked the US citizenship of women who married non–US citizens. However, the act did revoke the US citizenship of any woman who married people ineligible of US citizenship. This group included Japanese-born immigrants. Also in 1922, in a case known as *Ozawa v. United States*, the US Supreme Court ruled against a Japanese-born man who applied for naturalization after having lived most of his life in the United States. The court declared that because US immigration law did not specifically allow Japanese persons, he was ineligible due to his "Mongolian ancestry."

The Immigration Acts

Congress passed the Immigration Act of 1917 to add to the list of "undesirables" who would not be allowed to come into the country. Included on the list were "idiots, imbeciles, and feeble-minded persons," as well as epileptics, insane

Japanese demonstrators in Tokyo protest against the 1924 US immigration bill.

persons, alcoholics, people with infectious diseases such as tuberculosis, all persons "mentally or physically defective," polygamists, anarchists, contract laborers, the poor, and anyone "likely to be a burden" to the government. Another provision included a literacy test imposed on all persons over the age of sixteen. But the most controversial component of the act was the creation of the "Asiatic Barred Zone," which barred anyone entering the United States from "Any country not owned by the U.S. adjacent to the continent of Asia." This act was so offensive that President Woodrow Wilson vetoed it. However, Congress overwhelmingly overrode his veto.

After World War I ended in 1918, a wave of nationalism swept the country. The House Committee on Immigration and Naturalization began to investigate Japanese immigration, and in the summer of 1919, held preliminary hearings in the nation's capital about the perceived loss of jobs to Japanese immigrants.

The committee heard from Miller Freeman, leader of Washington's Anti-Japanese League, who said: "Today, in my opinion, the Japanese of our country look upon the Pacific coast really as nothing more than a colony of Japan, and the whites as a subject race." The director of the Veteran's Welfare Commission, Colonel W. M. Inglis, testified that when a Washington State sawmill was hiring, "The result was the Japanese were employed and the ex-service men were not."

In 1920, the committee met with leaders and citizens of the Western states in Seattle. In addition to Freeman and Inglis, other vocal attendees included representatives from the American Legion, Veterans of Foreign Wars, the Veterans Welfare Commission, and local immigration officials, farmers, and members of the local Japanese community. Organized labor and female citizens concerned about Japanese morality also gave testimony. The House committee concluded its Seattle meeting with a summary of other meetings held in Oregon and California and took its findings back to Washington, DC.

In 1924, with the leadership of Congressman Albert Johnson and Senator David Reed of Pennsylvania, Congress passed the Johnson-Reed Act, drastically reducing quotas for immigration. During the debate over the bill, Senator Ellison DuRant Smith of South Carolina declared, "Without offense, but with regard to the salvation of our own, let us shut the door and assimilate what we have, and let us breed pure American citizens and develop our own American resources."

Americans after World War I felt that immigration was raising the unemployment rate. A component of the Johnson-Reed Act called the National Origins Act changed the formula for determining how many persons from each country would be allowed into the United States. Instead of using the population of each nationality in the United States in 1910 as a basis for quotas, the new act determined quotas based on the 1890 census. Senator Reed explained that the former immigration law was too lenient. "It disregards entirely those of us who are interested in keeping American stock up to the highest standard—that is, the people who were born here," he said. The Johnson-Reed Act additionally excluded from entry anyone born in the "Asiatic Barred Zone." Within this immigration act was an act called the Japanese Exclusion Act. Quotas for Japanese immigrants were disallowed entirely. The justification for this was that Japanese nationals were unable to become naturalized citizens. After much going back and forth between the House, the Senate, and President Calvin Coolidge, the act was signed into law on May 26, 1924. According to the United States Office of the Historian, the act was created "to preserve the ideal of American homogeneity."

Setting the Stage

The news of the secret bombing of Pearl Harbor in late 1941 filled America's airwaves, sending fear and outrage across the nation. Congress and millions of Americans supported President Roosevelt's declaration of war. Thousands of young men lined up at military recruitment offices. As

America took its war stance, citizens also looked to the Japanese aliens on American soil with terror and distrust. It came to light quickly that many citizens wanted the Japanese removed. Those citizens who had been at the forefront of all the Japanese exclusion efforts were most prominent in urging the government to evacuate Japanese Americans. The government's eventual decision to arrest and imprison Japanese Americans was fortified by decades of resentment and suspicion—the exclusion movement, alien land laws, immigration prohibitions, and job and social discrimination.

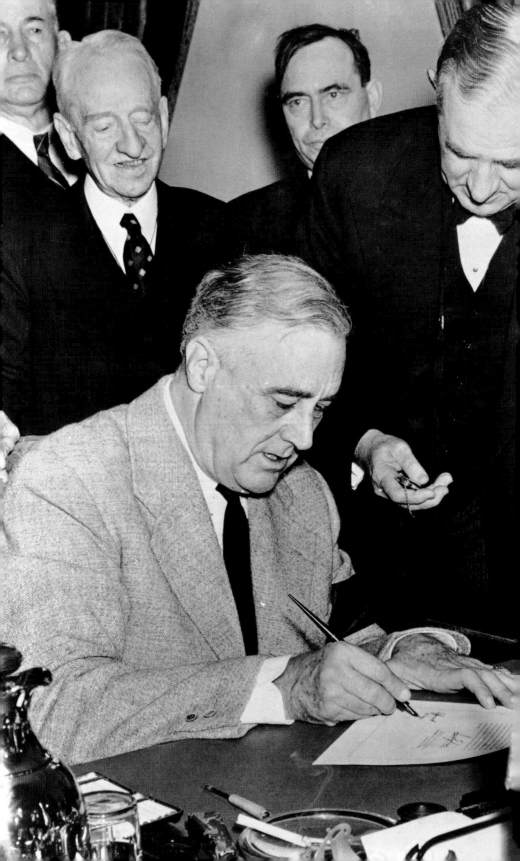

THREE

Forced Evacuation

O nce war was declared, people from many spheres — public, government, and business — demanded that the government banish the Japanese from America. This demand included not just immigrants but also native-born citizens. After Pearl Harbor, white Americans lashed out with untempered rage. The Veterans of Foreign Wars held an opinion shared by many when their leaders wrote to military officials "to emphatically urge that all Japanese, whether American-born or otherwise, be immediately removed." White citizens' long-held aversion toward Japanese Americans was most in evidence in the Western states — the Pacific coast and Arizona, Utah, Idaho, and Colorado.

Before there was a plan in place, bitter outpourings and media rants went completely unchecked. The cacophony of demonstrations, marches, posters, billboards, speeches, and radio and television broadcasts was almost boundless. The *Seattle Argus* newspaper, for instance, editorialized, "If the innocent are interned with the guilty, it will not be a very serious matter. If any Japs are allowed to remain at

Opposite: President Franklin D. Roosevelt signs the declaration of war against Japan.

large in this country, it might spell the greatest disaster in history." Even government officials held back nothing in their caustic remarks toward Japanese Americans. In Tennessee, for example, an irate citizen sent in a facetious request to the state Department of Conservation to request a hunting license "to hunt for Japanese invaders," and an official actually replied by writing, "No license required—Open season on Japs!" Congressman John Rankin of Mississippi declared:

> Do not forget that once a Japanese always a Japanese. I say it is of vital importance that we get rid of every Japanese whether in Hawaii or on the mainland. They violate every sacred promise, every canon of honor and decency. This was evidenced in their diplomacy and in their bombing of Hawaii. These Japs who had been there for generations were making signs, if you please, guiding the Japanese planes to the objects of their iniquity in order that they might destroy our naval vessels, murder our soldiers and sailors, and blow to pieces the helpless women and children of Hawaii. Damn them! Let us get rid of them now!

Fueled by such rhetoric, hysteria reigned after the attack on Pearl Harbor. Within days, the US government designated all Japanese Americans "4-C," meaning "enemy alien."

Race War

In the aftermath of Pearl Harbor, Lieutenant General John DeWitt, a trusted advisor to Franklin D. Roosevelt, declared,

A soldier posts the order for Bainbridge Island Japanese Americans to evacuate.

"In the war in which we are now engaged racial affinities are not severed by migration. The Japanese race is an enemy race and while many second and third generation Japanese born on United States soil, possessed of United States citizenship, have become 'Americanized,' the racial strains are undiluted."

The very indignation that Americans felt about the attack was testament to the fact that white Americans felt superior to the Japanese and that any success the Japanese had in outsmarting the United States was an appalling affront. Professor Gary Grestle, historian of World War II, wrote, "Japan's attack on the United States inflamed ingrained prejudices of white Americans ... The American-Japanese war in the Pacific, meanwhile, took on the coloration of a 'race-war' ... in which the two opposing sides engaged in a savage struggle to determine which race would triumph." A 1942 Gallup poll revealed that a majority of American citizens regarded the Japanese "as treacherous, sly, cruel, and warlike."

Although the United States was also at war with Germany and Italy, it was Japan that was the target of utter fury. After Pearl Harbor, many whites seized the opportunity to have "legitimate" reasons to discriminate. Besides an opportunity to express racial bitterness, white Americans also saw an opportunity to regain jobs they felt had been lost to Japanese workers. The head of a major California growers' association claimed, "If all of the Japs were removed tomorrow, we'd never miss them … because the white farmers can take over and produce everything the Jap grows." The truth of the statement is questionable because in 1940 the average value for farmland in America was approximately $38 per acre, while the average value for an acre of Japanese-owned farmland was approximately $275.

Sabotage

Americans were very willing to believe that Japanese Americans were likely spies. The unprecedented attack, which caught the US military intelligence by such surprise, was deemed impossible unless the Japanese on American soil were complicit. Lieutenant General DeWitt publically accused Japanese Americans of espionage. He believed that Japanese Americans were sending signals to Japanese submarines lurking off the Pacific coast. He warned the president not to assume that the Japanese in America would not turn against their adopted country when "the final test of loyalty comes." He believed the Japanese living along the Pacific coast were a **fifth column**, organizing and getting ready for action. (A fifth column is a group of people in a targeted area who assist in an external attack.) He said, "The very fact that no **sabotage** has taken place to date is a disturbing and confirming indication that such action will be taken."

In addition to DeWitt's accusations of treachery, there were claims that photo laboratories were developing film dropped off by Japanese Americans that contained images of bridges, manufacturing plants, highways, tunnels, and military defense sites.

President Franklin D. Roosevelt held suspicions that Japanese Americans could be capable of espionage. As far back as 1933, he commissioned a study from Army Intelligence to determine whether there was a threat in Hawaii because of the large population of Japanese Americans living there. The report noted that the Japanese had "racial traits" such as "moral inferiority to whites, fanaticism, duplicity, and arrogance." The study concluded that the Japanese Hawaiians were fiercely loyal to Japan and would be disloyal to the United States should there be war waged between the countries. Concerned about the large number of Japanese ships that came to port in Hawaii, President Roosevelt wrote, "One obvious thought occurs to me—that every Japanese citizen or non-citizen on the Island of Oahu who meets these Japanese ships or has any connection with their officers or men should be secretly but definitely identified and his or her name placed on a special list of those who would be the first to be placed in a concentration camp in the event of trouble."

Beliefs Baseless

Before the United States entered the war, the president worried he did not have enough intelligence about Japanese Americans. And due to the failing relations between Japan and the United States, he asked a journalist friend, John

Carter, to prepare a report on those of Japanese ancestry residing in the country. In particular, he wanted a report on those residing on the Pacific coast. Carter hired an investigator named Curtis Munsen, a midwestern businessman who had conducted other investigative work for the president.

In his first report, Munsen wrote, "We do not want to throw a lot of American citizens into a concentration camp of course, and especially as the almost unanimous verdict is that in case of war they will be quiet, very quiet … There will probably be some sabotage by paid Japanese agents and the odd fanatical Jap, but the bulk of these people will be quiet because in addition to being quite contented with the American Way of life, they know they are 'in a spot.'" His later reports continued in the same vein; he concluded that the Japanese were "certified a remarkable, even extraordinary degree of loyalty among this generally suspect ethnic group."

He also believed that in the event of war, the Japanese Americans would suffer a greater violence from the hands of white Americans than the reverse. He went on the say that "the Nisei are pathetically eager to show this loyalty. They are not Japanese in culture. They are foreigners to Japan." He also reported that in Hawaii, nearly 98 percent of Japanese residents were loyal to the United States, and those that were deemed otherwise were being closely monitored by the Federal Bureau of Investigation (FBI) and the navy. On December 2, just days away from the Pearl Harbor attack, he told the president that the Japanese Americans in both Hawaii and on the mainland were "considerably weakened in their loyalty to Japan by the fact that they have chosen to make this their home and have brought up their children here. They expect to die here." His final report concluded, "The Japanese are hampered as saboteurs because of their easily recognized physical appearance. It will be hard for them to get near anything to blow up if it is guarded … As interview after interview piled up, those bringing in results began to call it the same old tune. The story was all the same. There is no Japanese 'problem' on the Coast. There will be no armed uprising of Japanese."

Unfortunately, the report prepared by Munsen was presented to the president along with a one-page summary from John Carter, which included items out of context such as "There will be the odd case of fanatical sabotage by some Japanese 'crackpot.' There are still Japanese in the United States who will tie dynamite around their waist and make a human bomb, but today they are few." Carter left out "paid Japanese agents," giving the impression any Japanese American could be suspect.

Even after December 7, official reports continued to emphasize that Japanese Americans were neither disloyal nor potential spies. Naval Lieutenant Commander K. D. Ringle sent a memo to the chief of naval operations, in part saying, "In short, the entire 'Japanese Problem' has been magnified out of its true proportion, largely because of the physical characteristics of the people; that it is no more serious than the problems of the German, Italian, and Communistic portions of the United States population, and, finally that it should be handled on the basis of the individual, regardless of citizenship, and not on a racial basis."

Immediate Reactions

After the bombing, the US government immediately placed Hawaii under martial law. As Hawaii was the first target, many concluded any number of the more than 150,000 Japanese residents of Hawaii could have been abettors. But no more than 1,500 Japanese aliens, along with some Italian and German aliens, were immediately taken into custody. Some were released, but most were sent to detention camps. The American plantation owners feared that continued arrests of Japanese workers would destroy the economy. As a result, the military assigned the planters responsibility for their own security. Because of this, a comparatively few Japanese Americans in Hawaii were detained or interned.

Soon after, the Japanese navy captured two islands off the coast of Alaska, giving rise to government fears that the West Coast was the next target. Lieutenant General DeWitt, now commander of the Western Defense Command, ordered the removal of "all alien subjects fourteen years of age and over." He later reconsidered his policy of arresting all Japanese Americans, saying, "We are going to have an awful job on our hands and are very liable to alienate the local Japanese ... An American citizen, after all, is an American citizen." DeWitt formed the Wartime Civil Control Administration, which was given the task of establishing security zones from which any person could be excluded. The restrictions were enforced mainly on Japanese Americans. Said one official, "I have little confidence that the enemy aliens are law-abiding or loyal ... Particularly the Japanese. I have no confidence in their loyalty whatsoever."

Lieutenant General John DeWitt called for internment.

In January, DeWitt listed eighty-six security zones. Those residing or working in the zones had to relocate. He also requested that others voluntarily relocate to interior states. Governors of such states protested. Idaho governor Chase Clark said that Japanese Americans could come to Idaho only if they were in "concentration camps under military guard." Further pressure from citizens convinced DeWitt that mass removal should be put in place. Officials in the Wartime Civil Control Administration sought the support of California attorney general Earl Warren, who demanded DeWitt take harsher action.

Thereafter, DeWitt ordered, "All enemy aliens and Japanese-Americans in the western halves of California, Oregon and Washington, and in the southern half of Arizona will be placed under rigid new curfew regulations Friday, and any violators will be immediately punished." FBI agents began conducting searches of Japanese American homes. People were forced to give up "contraband," such as radios, flashlights, diaries, Japanese-language books, Japanese-English dictionaries, books with maps, plastic or toy weapons, and rifles. Many possessing those items were arrested. Strict travel restrictions were put into place, as well as restrictions on work hours and social gatherings. Strict curfews were also imposed. Agents arrested prominent leaders in Japanese communities—teachers in language schools, priests, community organizers, radio broadcasters, and newspaper editors. They were often arrested in the middle of the night and taken to secret locations.

Executive Order 9066

By January 1942, citizens demanded that the government remove Japanese Americans for reasons of national security. Assistant Secretary of War John J. McCloy received approval for mass removal of enemy aliens from Secretary of War Henry Stimson and the president on February 11. On February 19, 1942, President Roosevelt signed **Executive Order 9066**, which called for the exclusion and internment of anyone considered a danger to national security. Although some Germans and Italians were arrested, the true focus of the order was against Japanese Americans.

The order itself called on the "Secretary of War, and the Military Commanders whom he may from time to time designate, ... to prescribe military areas in such places and of such extent as he or the appropriate Military Commander may determine, from which any or all persons may be excluded." It then authorized the secretary of war and other governmental leaders "to provide for residents of any such area who are excluded therefrom, such transportation, food, shelter, and other accommodations as may be necessary ... including the furnishing of medical aid, hospitalization, food, clothing, transportation, use of land, shelter, and other supplies, equipment, utilities, facilities and services."

The only person close to the president who disagreed was his wife, Eleanor Roosevelt, who believed the order was a reaction to hysteria and anxiety, saying, "These people were not convicted of any crime but emotions ran too high, too many people wanted to wreak vengeance on Oriental looking people." Future US Senator Daniel Inouye, a decorated veteran who was born in Hawaii and witnessed the attack on Pearl Harbor, said, "It took no great effort of imagination to see the hatred of many Americans for the enemy turned on us, who looked so much like him."

Consequences

Throughout the West, relocation notices containing the text of Executive Order 9066 were posted onto buildings, telephone poles, and any other public area in Japanese American neighborhoods. All people of Japanese ancestry, including those who were only one-sixteenth Japanese, were required to register. The order required that each Japanese head of household report to army civil control stations to register before evacuation. The evacuees needed to provide all personal information, such as education, occupation, and alien registration number, as well as physical condition of each family member. People were given one to three weeks to register, pack, and sell or rent their homes, businesses, farms, equipment, and other valuables.

Bargain hunters stood at the ready to take advantage of the distress sales. Supposedly, federal agencies were available to advise and protect the evacuees, to help them "cope with the multitude of problems involved in suddenly cutting off the normal business, social and economic relationships," but little help was really provided. Everywhere there were signs, "Evacuation Sale," "One Day to Go," or "50 Percent Off."

Farmers looked to their neighbors to tend their crops, some with success, most without. The California Evacuated Farms Association of the US Farm Security Administration helped white farmers purchase farms belonging to the Japanese Americans using "special" loans. Families lost their houses and businesses. Japanese American business owners who owned real estate in cities also lost their property to whites with the help of government agencies. The mayor of Los Angeles said, "Property within this city formerly occupied or used by the Japanese will not remain idle or fall into a state of disrepair." Victims reported getting cents on the dollar for their belongings—a new pickup truck sold for $25, a house for $500, $400 pianos sold for $5, new

refrigerators and stoves sold for $10 or $15. One farmer sold his large farm, equipment, greenhouse, and crops for $2,000. The buyer promptly resold all of it for $10,000. Fishers lost boats, tackle, and their canneries.

Japanese Americans were forced to sell their homes, businesses, and belongings at drastically reduced prices.

People were told to surrender anything that might be used to communicate with the enemy. The San Francisco Police Department alone reported it collected six thousand radios and cameras. The evacuees were allowed to take only the belongings they could carry. Personal items allowed were bed linen, a few changes of clothing, eating utensils, and toilet articles. The Japanese Americans were confused and disbelieving, although cooperative. James Sakamoto, editor of the *Japanese-American Courier*, wrote:

> No matter what develops involving the United States in the present tragic world situation, we Americans of Japanese ancestry must be prepared and remember that there are certain fundamental truths from which we cannot depart. One of them is that we were born in these United States as American citizens … We will stand firm in our resolution that even if America may 'disown' us—we will never 'disown' America.

Assembly Centers

Relocation camps were still incomplete at the time Executive Order 9066 was being implemented. Persons were rounded up and ordered onto trains that would carry them to one of fifteen temporary **assembly centers** constructed in stadiums, racetracks, and fairgrounds. People were housed in former livestock pens or horse stalls, or cheaply constructed barracks. The Western Defense Command posted "Civilian Exclusion Orders," (CEOs) informing each of 108 Japanese neighborhoods of their evacuation dates. The earliest CEOs were in communities nearest to sensitive military areas. The first CEO was posted on March 24, 1942, ordering fifty-five Japanese fishing and farming families on Bainbridge Island, near Seattle, to prepare for evacuation. They were given six days to dispense with their belongings, pack, and say good-bye to their mostly sympathetic friends and neighbors. On March 30, under armed guard, the evacuees were put on a ferry and began their journey to an assembly center in Manzanar, in Central California. Soldiers reported the people were cooperative, though resigned to their fate. After the 227 residents of Bainbridge Island were removed, the government went about the business of moving more than 120,000 persons of Japanese ancestry, many of them American citizens.

Many persons were detained at assembly centers for as long three months before being assigned to an internment camp. Upon arrival, each person underwent a physical, and families were assigned a barracks. Baggage was inspected for contraband. Families were assigned barracks measuring at most 200 square feet (18 square meters). In Tulare, one of the assembly centers, living spaces measured 8 square feet (0.74 sq m) per person. In the assembly center at the Western Washington Fairgrounds (nicknamed "Camp Harmony"), people were assigned housing in livestock pens. At the Tanforan assembly center, six people were assigned to live in a horse stall which had originally housed a single racehorse. Each "apartment" had cots for sleeping, blankets, and a lightbulb. People ate in mess halls. Communal bathrooms

Bainbridge Island Japanese Americans board the train in Seattle for the assembly center in Manzanar, California.

had no partitions between toilets and showers. Sanitation was substandard, as was the food, and most everyone was malnourished or otherwise ill. The Wartime Civil Control Administration employed evacuees whenever possible to reduce costs. Internees worked in kitchens, latrines, laundries, or sometimes in the fields growing crops. Inmates were also given a monthly coupon to purchase personal items such as clothing. Children under sixteen received $1 a month; people older received $2.50. No family could receive more than $7.50.

Internment Camps

The War Relocation Authority (WRA) set up ten internment camps in isolated and desolate locations in California, Arizona, Colorado, Idaho, Utah, Wyoming, and Arkansas. Guards kept an eye on the camps from watchtowers; fences were made of barbed wire. Each was its own community with schools, hospitals, shops, factories, agriculture fields, and a quasi-democratic government. Just as in the assembly centers, people were assigned tiny barracks with cots, blankets, and a lightbulb. The barracks had no plumbing or running water, and were heated in winter by small wood stoves. Those people that passed muster worked in the camps but received very little pay. Most people used what savings they had from the sale of their possessions to make life a bit more comfortable. The Issei were unable to do so, however, because their assets and bank accounts had been frozen by the federal government.

The internment camps located in the desert faced extreme temperature changes—scorching hot in summer and snowy and cold in winter. People were also exposed to wild swings in temperature day to night. Wind howled across the desolate landscape and dust storms were frequent. Some internees dug deep trenches alongside their barracks to rest in and get away from the heat and dust. One Manzanar resident said, "Oh, it's really so hot, you see, and the wind blows. There is no shade at all. It's miserable, really." The housing was cheap— tar paper over thin plywood walls—and provided no relief in summer or winter. Prior to their evacuation, the internees had lived along the Pacific coast, where the climate was mild to moderate, so much of their clothing was inadequate for their new climate. To add to the misery, they were fed a diet mainly of starches such as potatoes and bread, which gave rise to malnourishment and food poisoning. Poor sanitation and close quarters led to epidemics of dysentery, typhoid, and smallpox. Hospitals were understaffed and underfunded.

The Japanese internees lived under armed guard. There were curfews as well as roll calls twice daily. Military police could enter all buildings and barracks at any time without a warrant or any notice. Visitors were heavily screened, and mail and parcels were opened and inspected. As each new train arrived, and more evacuees disembarked, people on the inside watched for the newcomers and looked for familiar faces. As internee Mary Tsukamoto described, "We saw all these people behind the fence, looking out, hanging onto the wire, and looking out because they were anxious to know who was coming in. But I will never forget the shocking feeling that human beings were behind this fence like animals and crying. And we were going to also lose our freedom and walk inside of that gate and find ourselves … cooped up there … When the gates were shut, we knew that we had lost something that was very precious; that we were no longer free."

The government did not provide adequately for schools or other services. The inmates, through their own initiative, organized and managed schools, libraries, churches, and adult education classes. They published newspapers, planted gardens, and offered recreational opportunities such as flower arranging and baseball. Speaking and writing in the Japanese language, in nearly all situations, was forbidden.

George Takei, the Hollywood actor who has performed in numerous television shows and movies and may be best known as Mr. Sulu of the *Star Trek* television series, was evacuated to a concentration camp at the age of five. In an interview he stated:

Shikata ga nai

Shikata ga nai is a Japanese expression meaning, "It can't be helped; that's the way it is." Acceptance of authority was the prevailing attitude of the internees. Resistance and protest were basically foreign to Japanese culture.

Trusting that their adopted country would do them no lasting harm, the internees, confused and frightened, boarded trains under armed guard for the internment camps. All but the swamp-filled Arkansas camps were in a barren desert, surrounded by barbed wire and dotted with tarpaper barracks. Japanese people value modesty, which was lost when whole families were assigned a single room. The rooms had a potbellied stove and a light bulb, and each person had a cot and a mattress stuffed with straw. People hung bits of cloth or rice sacks to separate sleeping quarters and scavenged for wooden crates to make furniture. There was no insulation—summer brought temperatures above 100 degrees Fahrenheit (38 degrees Celsius), and in winter temperatures plunged below freezing. Cracks in the walls gave little protection against wind, sand, and snow. Sandstorms were particularly grueling. Betty Chin, an internee, recalled, "The sand is so blinding. You'd have to get your head down and run but you don't really know where you are."

In the morning, the residents of each block—generally about two hundred fifty people—waited in lines to use the communal bathrooms. One internee recalled, "The thing about using the toilet was once in a while the food wasn't just right and

Swirling sands pass through the paper-thin walls of the barracks at the Manzanar internment camp.

everybody got the runs and oh god, because they all got diarrhea they lined up. It was really something."

People ate in mess halls. The camps were supposed to produce much of their own food and be self-sufficient, but the desert soil and climate often made that a challenge. With vegetables and meat frequently absent from menus, people were fed mostly rice and other starches. Masaru Kawaguchi, an internee at Topaz, remembered, "The food was something terrible. Life revolves around the mess hall time because if you don't eat at that time you don't get fed. In the mornings they ring a bell and everybody goes in and gets in a line to eat breakfast—and the same thing happens at noon and the same thing happens in the evening. So most of the time you listen for the bell."

However dehumanizing the camps were, and despite being guarded by armed soldiers, the internees tried to live normal lives. People married and had children; they celebrated birthdays and holidays. They built makeshift schools and churches, baseball fields and basketball courts. Many Japanese teachers, religious leaders, doctors, nurses, food service workers, farmers, carpenters, and sanitation workers were hired to work for only a few dollars a day, but without their contributions, life in the camps would have been far more dismal.

We're Americans. We were citizens of this country. We had nothing to do with the war. We simply happened to look like the people that bombed Pearl Harbor. But without charges, without trial, without due process—the fundamental pillar of our justice system—we were summarily rounded up, all Japanese Americans on the West Coast, where we were primarily resident, and sent off to ten barbed wire internment camps—prison camps, really, with sentry towers, machine guns pointed at us—in some of the most desolate places in this country: the wastelands of Wyoming, Idaho, Utah, Colorado, the blistering hot desert of Arizona, of all places, in black tarpaper barracks. And our family was sent two-thirds of the way across the country, the farthest east, in the swamps of Arkansas. I could see the barbed wire fence and the sentry towers right outside my schoolhouse window as I recited the words "with liberty and justice for all," an innocent child unaware of the irony.

People were divided into categories—the Issei, Nisei, **Sansei** (children born of Nisei and also American citizens), and **Kibei** (second-generation Japanese Americans with citizenship who attended school in Japan). Especially in the first year, there were many demonstrations and strikes conducted mostly by Nisei and Kibei, who were enraged at the living conditions and the abuse of their constitutional rights as citizens. The WRA and the WCCA removed the "troublemakers" and sent them to high-security prison camps—

Tule Lake, a segregation camp; Moab, Utah, a rehabilitation center; or Leupp, Arizona, an isolation center.

The Questionnaire

On February 1, 1943, the army decided to induct Japanese Americans into military service. They wanted to register all young men for the draft and to form segregated combat teams. They also planned to draft English-Japanese interpreters and code breakers. All inmates seventeen years of age and older were given a questionnaire designed to test their loyalty to the United States. Most of the form addressed family connections, education, religion, skills, club memberships, and property ownership. Each person's form was scored according to how "American" or "Japanese" their answers were. For example, if a person spoke Japanese well or subscribed to Japanese-language magazines or newspapers, those were negative. If he or she practiced martial arts or Buddhism or Shinto, again that would tally as a negative. However, if a person belonged to the girl or boy scouts or was a Christian, he or she was awarded positive points.

The problematic questions most people objected to were loyalty questions numbers 25 through 28. The most serious were numbers 27 and 28. Question 27 asked, "Are you willing to serve in the armed forces of the United States on combat duty, wherever ordered?" Question 28 asked, "Will you swear unqualified allegiance to the United States of America and faithfully defend the United States from any and all attacks by foreign and domestic forces, and forswear any form of allegiance or disobedience to the

Internment Facts

There were between 110,000 and 120,000 Japanese Americans sent to internment camps, known as relocation centers, between May 8 and October 6, 1942. Two-thirds of those incarcerated were US citizens, and an estimated half of them were children. Here is a list of the incarceration camps and their peak populations.

Camp	Peak Population
Topaz, UT	8,130
Colorado River, AZ	17,814
Gila River AZ	13,348
Granada, CO	7,318
Heart Mountain, WY	10,767
Jerome, AR	8,497
Manzanar, CA	10,046
Minidoka, ID	9,397
Rohwer, AR	8,475
Tule Lake, CA	18,789
Total peak incarceration	120,711

There were sixteen assembly centers of Japanese Americans. In alphabetical order they were located at: Fresno, CA; Manzanar, CA; Marysville, CA; Mayer, AZ; Merced, CA; Pinedale, CA; Pomona, CA; Portland, OR; Sacramento, CA; Puyallup, WA; Salinas, CA; Santa Anita, CA; Stockton, CA; Tanforan, CA; Tulare, CA; and Turlock, CA.

There were four Department of Justice camps for "troublemakers" who were not American citizens: Santa Fe, NM; Bismarck, ND; Crystal City, TX; Missoula, MT.

There were two citizen isolation camps for "troublemakers" and military resistors who were American citizens: Moab, UT; Leupp, AZ.

There were 4,724 people expatriated to Japan.

Japanese Emperor, or any other foreign government, power, or organization?" Young Nisei and Kibei men resented that they were being asked to volunteer for the army without the promise of regaining any civil rights. Most felt the same as Masaru Kawaguchi, an internee in the Topaz internment camp, who said, "They decided that we were now going to be drafted into service. Can you imagine that? Here you're in jail, and they said you're going to be drafted into the service!" Question 28 was even more concerning. For many Japanese Americans, being asked to renounce loyalty to Japan when they never had any loyalty to Japan was a double-edged sword. Additionally, as the Issei had been denied US citizenship, should they choose to forgo their Japanese citizenship they would be left stateless.

Young men who answered "no" to both questions 27 and 28 were known as "No-No Boys," and thus ineligible to leave the camps or join the armed forces. In some quarters, the "No-No Boys" were considered shameful; in others they were heroes. The questionnaire's results divided people into loyal or disloyal categories. Those who tested disloyal, in particular the "No-No Boys," were sent to the segregation center at Tule Lake to join three thousand inmates there who refused to complete the questionnaire altogether. All told, more than twelve thousand "No-No Boys" were imprisoned at Tule Lake and other high security centers. More than three thousand people, mostly Issei and Kibei, asked to be **repatriated** to Japan.

However, more than thirty-three thousand Nisei and Kibei joined the military. Many, especially the Kibei who were not trained as soldiers but were fluent in Japanese, served in military intelligence and risked their lives in combat zones to translate during interrogations of prisoners of war. Nisei, most of whom did not speak Japanese, were assigned to segregated regiments. Senator Inouye was among them. His regiment fought in France and Italy, where Inouye lost his right arm. He was awarded a Distinguished Service Cross that was later upgraded to a Medal of Honor by President Bill Clinton, a Bronze Star, and a Purple Heart for his heroism. The senator said that he dropped out of medical school when the army began accepting Japanese Americans and enlisted. He recalled his leave-taking: "My father just looked straight ahead, and I looked straight ahead, and then he cleared his throat and said, 'America has been good to us. It has given me two jobs. It has given you and your sisters and brothers education. We all love this country. Whatever you do, do not dishonor your country. Remember—never dishonor your family. And if you must give your life, do so with honor.' I knew exactly what he meant. I said, 'Yes, sir. Good-bye.'"

Japanese American soldiers fought on the ground against Japanese troops in many areas, including in the brutal battles in the jungles of Myanmar (Burma). Speaking of his service there, a soldier named Dick Hamada said, "Being in a jungle, being that we possess the face of an enemy, I was very much afraid of people that I didn't know. I was safe with my people, Americans ... But there are other people that you would run with during your campaign that didn't know who you were. And that was what I was afraid of. I was afraid of being shot by them. So an American always [accompanied] me wherever I went. That's for safety."

The military warned the Nisei that if captured, the Japanese would be ruthless with them as prisoners of war. Hamada recalled, "I was instructed to keep one bullet for myself in the event I should get captured." The all–Japanese American 442nd regiment, in which Inouye served, was the most decorated regiment in the war. Among its many honors was a Congressional Medal of Honor. In one of its major battles, it rescued a Texas battalion lost inside enemy territory. The state of Texas, in gratitude, restored civil rights to the soldiers of the 442nd and gave them "Texas citizenship."

Hemispheric Security

The United States was not alone in its fear and rejection of the Japanese living inside its borders. After Pearl Harbor, the Canadian government passed "Order in Council PC 1486" allowing the Minister of Justice to remove Japanese Canadians living within 100 miles (160 kilometers) of Canada's Pacific coast. On March 4, 1942, twenty-two thousand Japanese

Canadians were ordered to pack their belongings and be ready for removal the following day. Initially, the Japanese Canadians were housed in a temporary facility—the Hastings Park racetrack. Men were taken from their families and sent to work building roads, bridges, and railroads, as well as laboring in sugar beet fields. Women, children, and the elderly were sent to several internment camps located in remote farming areas or ghost towns in British Columbia's interior. Some who wanted to operate farms instead of going to work on a work crew actually paid for their own removal and imprisonment. Men who protested or broke curfew were sent to prisoner of war camps in Ontario and forced to wear prison shirts with red targets on their backs. Due to the sudden removal of Japanese Canadians, the people were unable to sell their belongings or lease their property. They returned to nothing. Japanese Canadians were not allowed to return to the West Coast until 1949.

Latin America

In 1893, Japan was interested in going abroad to establish colonies, as Europeans had done. The government wanted to acquire not only natural resources but also land in order to encourage emigration from their overpopulated nation. A group of officials formed the Colonization Society and in 1897 attempted to establish an agricultural colony in Mexico. It was not successful, but the society continued its mission into other parts of Latin America. The first group of emigrants went to Peru. As the United States began curtailing Japanese immigration, more Japanese citizens immigrated to the Latin

American countries of Argentina, Bolivia, Brazil, Chile, Colombia, Costa Rica, Cuba, Ecuador, El Salvador, Mexico, Nicaragua, Peru, Panama, Paraguay, and Venezuela.

Even before Pearl Harbor, President Franklin D. Roosevelt was concerned about "hemispheric security." He worried that Axis powers in Latin America would pose a threat to the United States. He was not confident that the governments in South and Central America, as well as Mexico, would be able to control their alien population. So he sent FBI agents to US embassies to look for subversive behavior. After war was declared, the president ordered the US Immigration and Naturalization Service (INS) to construct prison camps in New Mexico, Louisiana, and Texas. He pressured Latin American countries to deport their "enemy aliens" to the United States, including diplomats. When the deportees arrived in the United States, they were without passports or visas, thus officially authorizing the INS to detain and intern them. (Chile and Argentina refused to deport the Japanese as they were fearful of attack from Japan and did not want to break off relations.) Mexico did not deport many Japanese residents to the United States, but the government evacuated all those living within 124 miles (200 km) of the Pacific coast and 62 miles (100 km) of the United States-Mexico border. They ordered the Japanese inland to Mexico City and Guadalajara. Also interned at the INS camps were Axis sailors who were aboard ships anchored in US harbors.

FOUR

Speaking Out

As hysteria rose and propaganda against Japanese Americans reached a crescendo, a few individuals tried to be heard above the noise. "Anti-Japanese propaganda," wrote Carey McWilliams, "has always been characterized by its offensive stupidity." An author of numerous books and magazine articles in the *Nation, Harper's,* and the *New Republic,* McWilliams also ran California's Division of Immigration and Housing. As California edged toward the mass incarceration of its many Japanese American citizens and residents, McWilliams called it "a tragic mistake, shameful and unnecessary … and certainly the most serious violation of civil liberties in this century."

He argued against the decision, saying of the mass removal, "The mess that is being made of this Japanese situation simply beggars description." After leaving office in 1944, McWilliams published a book titled *Prejudice: Japanese-Americans: Symbol of Racial Intolerance.* In the

Opposite: First Lady Eleanor Roosevelt visits school children at the Gila River internment camp.

book, he not only called for reparations to those incarcerated but for the federal government to forbid future discrimination based on race, color, creed, or national origin.

Archibald MacLeish won the Pulitzer Prize for poetry in 1932. He was also an editor and writer for the business magazine *Fortune*. A friend of President Roosevelt, MacLeish was appointed head of the federal Office of Facts and Figures, a new government agency, in 1941. His job was to oversee the authenticity of war coverage by newspapers, radio, and film, and to advise on censorship issues. He also reviewed radio speeches, articles, and other wartime propaganda efforts. Independent of his assignment, he encouraged Japanese-language radio and newspapers to stay abreast of the events that were going to affect them. MacLeish went to the West Coast and tried to calm the hysterical news coverage by broadcasters and publishers. He beseeched Hollywood screenwriters to make pro-Japanese statements. Upon his return, he urged the deputy secretary of war to avoid making a rash decision based on pressure from agricultural organizations and racist groups.

In 1942, Bob Fletcher, a Sacramento state agricultural inspector, took it upon himself to rescue Japanese farmers after Executive Order 9066. He quit his job and took over management of farms belonging to three Japanese families in Sacramento. He cultivated 90 acres (36 hectares) of grapes. With the proceeds of the crop, he paid the Japanese farmers' mortgages and taxes and saved half of the profits for the families for when they returned. In an interview in 2010, he said, "I did know a few of them pretty well and never agreed with the evacuation. They were the same as anybody else. It was obvious they had nothing to do with Pearl Harbor." Despite being taunted by the rest of the community, even to the degree that shots were fired into his barn, he held onto the farms and returned them to their original owners after the camps closed. Of his action, he said, "It was the right thing to do."

In 1940, a young couple, Walt and Milly Woodward, bought a community newspaper called the *Bainbridge Review* on Bainbridge Island, Washington. On the first day of publication, they promised to "always strive to speak the truth, unafraid, whether it be on a national issue or something purely local." The island had a fair-sized Japanese American population, most of whom were farmers or fishers. When Executive Order 9066 came out, the Woodwards wasted no time speaking their minds. First they warned, "There is the danger of a blind, wild hysterical hatred of all persons who can trace ancestry to Japan. That some of those persons happen to be American citizens ... easily could be swept aside by mob hysteria." They reminded citizens that "These Japanese Americans of ours haven't bombed anybody ... They have given every indication of loyalty to this nation. They have sent ... their own sons into the United States Army." The Woodwards barely eked out a living from their newspaper, but as their editorials continued their anti-evacuation stance, they lost numerous advertisers and subscribers. Bainbridge Island was the first community to be evacuated under Executive Order 9066. Japanese Americans were given less than a week to part with their belongings

Photographer Dorothea Lange showed how bleak life was in the internment camps. Nearly eight hundred of her photographs were banned by the government.

and pack what personal items they were allowed. The *Bainbridge Review* was the only newspaper in the nation to be consistently and emphatically against internment. After the island's Japanese residents were evacuated, the Woodwards hired four Japanese American high school students as "Camp Correspondents" to write articles about life at Manzanar and Minidoka for the newspaper.

The Power of Imagery

Not all protestors used words. Some used images. Photographer Dorothea Lange was hired by the US government to chronicle the activities of the Farm Security Administration, Office of War Information, and the War Relocation Authority. Her biographer wrote, "What the military wanted from her was a set of photographs to illustrate that they weren't persecuting or torturing these people who they evacuated." But a brochure from a Library of Congress exhibition stated, "Lange's photographs reveal the plight of internees forced to leave their lives and homes behind … Lange created images that frequently juxtapose signs of human courage and dignity with physical evidence of the indignities of incarceration." She photographed what she saw—people waiting in line; plain, shoddy barracks; barbed wire; and the cold and dust of remote locations. More than eight hundred of Lange's photographs were "impounded" by the government. She was fired in July 1942. Lange wrote of her experience, "This is what we did. How did it happen? How could we?"

Toyo Miyatake, a Los Angeles photographer and gallery owner, was himself an internee. During his internment, his photographs were published without giving him credit. The byline was only "Associated Press." His photograph "Boys Behind Barbed Wire" is one of the most iconic images of the internment.

Ansel Adams was a high profile photographer known for Western landscapes. In 1943, the warden of Manzanar invited him to take photographs, ostensibly to show that Japanese American internees were being well treated. He was not supposed to photograph the barbed wire, watchtowers, and guards. Adams did not photograph them directly, but they could be viewed indirectly—such as the shadow of a soldier, or the high wall of a guard tower. Barbed wire could be seen as a blur in the distance or out of focus in the foreground of

Angered by Racism

Hugh Macbeth, a graduate of Harvard Law School, was the founding editor of the *Baltimore Times*. He later moved to Los Angeles, where he settled in a mostly Japanese American neighborhood. In 1938, the California governor appointed Macbeth as a commissioner and executive secretary of the newly formed Race Relations Commission. He was the sole African American on the commission. After Executive Order 9066, Macbeth interviewed several Issei who had been among the first group to be evacuated. He learned that most were prosperous farmers and not saboteurs. Angered by the racism and greed of white farmers, Macbeth organized several church and pro-Japanese groups to petition the government to oppose removal of Japanese Americans. He was concerned that families were being "torn up by the roots" and sent from their homes to "they know not where."

Led by Macbeth, the California Race Relations Commission and the Santa Barbara Minister's Alliance were the only Southern California organizations to officially oppose evacuation. Macbeth sent telegrams to the president and General DeWitt, asking them to allow Japanese farmers to continue their work. He was co-counsel for Ernest and Toki Wakayama, who filed **habeas corpus petitions**. In 1944, he signed the Japanese American Citizens League brief for *Korematsu v. United States*. In February 1945, he represented Fred and Kajiro Oyama and argued that the state's Alien Land Law penalized the Japanese American farmers by being based solely on race. The case ultimately came before the Supreme Court, which struck down the law. In 1945, Macbeth hired Chiyoko Sakamoto, the first Nisei woman lawyer in the state, when, after her release from internment, she was unable to find a job.

a photo. In 1944, he published his work as *Born Free and Equal: The Story of Loyal Japanese-Americans*. He wrote, "The purpose of my work was to show how these people, suffering under a great injustice, and loss of property, businesses and professions, had overcome the sense of defeat and despair."

Groups and Organizations

The groups that most reliably supported the Japanese were church groups. The American Baptist Home Mission Society encouraged their faithful to reject the propaganda against Japanese Americans. They published a national pamphlet in 1944 entitled *Democracy Demands Fair Play for America's Japanese*. One spread of the pamphlet shows excerpts from newspapers with a banner reading, "Leading Papers Speak Up For It." The other spread, titled "The People Practice It," features a page of photographs showing Japanese Americans working and playing alongside white Americans. The church lobbied the government for release. They stored the Japanese Americans' belongings in church basements and parishioners' homes and sent supplies and missionaries to the camps.

The Colorado Council of Churches published a booklet, titled *The Japanese in Our Midst*, aimed at dispelling the propaganda and spreading the idea of tolerance and understanding. Many churches gathered at national conventions and backed resolutions calling for the rights of the internees to be reinstated. The American Friends Services Committee, affiliated with the Quakers, established a program called National Japanese American Student Relocation Council, which helped Japanese American college students transfer to "safe" colleges in the East. Several major charitable foundations contributed. Eventually, more than 4,300 college students left the camps to attend school. The Friends also provided clothing, books, and recreational equipment to the internees.

Public Figures

When Executive Order 9066 was announced, the governor of Colorado, Ralph Carr, said, "This is a difficult time for all Japanese-speaking people. We must work together for the preservation of our American system and the continuation of our theory of universal brotherhood ... If we do not extend humanity's kindness and understanding to [the Japanese Americans], if we deny them the protection of the Bill of Rights, if we say that they must be denied the privilege of living in any of the forty-eight states without hearing or charge of misconduct, then we are tearing down the whole American system."

His stance was not popular, and he was the only Western governor to reject the policy of evacuation. He invited

Governor Ralph Carr of Colorado was the sole Western governor to speak against the internment.

Japanese evacuees to move to Colorado. At a ceremony later honoring him, it was said he "rolled up his sleeves on the side of the angels and helped the Japanese-Americans regain respectability."

When President Roosevelt issued Executive Order 9066, one of his biggest detractors was his wife, Eleanor Roosevelt. The First Lady could not appear to be interfering with the operation of the government, but she did let her opinions be known. She praised the patriotism of the Nisei who enlisted and posed with them in pictures. After Pearl Harbor, she discovered that the Treasury Department had frozen the bank accounts of "enemy aliens." She had the order partially rescinded, giving the Issei access to one hundred dollars a month. On a national radio broadcast in January 1942, she said, "The Issei may be aliens technically, but in reality they are Americans and America has a place for all loyal persons regardless of race or citizenship." She used money from her special projects fund to provide emergency aid and contributed to the student relocation program. The First Lady also visited the Gila River internment camp and extended her sympathy to internees. She urged Americans to "live up to traditional American ideals of fairness."

Under Protest

Although many lived by the motto, "Do not be the nail sticking up," some Japanese Americans did protest their evacuation, the camp conditions, and the military draft. The Heart Mountain Fair Play Committee was an organization whose members were draft-age Nisei men interned at Heart Mountain in Wyoming. They advocated for the reinstatement of their civil rights as a precondition for signing up for the draft. On March 6, 1944, young men began refusing to report for their physical examinations. Although many internees disagreed with them, fearing for the men's safety as well as anticipating reprisals against themselves, by the end of June, sixty-three young men from Heart Mountain and twenty-two from the Poston camp had refused to take their physicals. They were tried in federal district court and sentenced to three years each in a federal penitentiary. Later that year, they lost an appeal of their case.

Tule Lake operated under strict martial law as a high-security segregation center. Here, many of the "No-No Boys" were imprisoned, as well as others whom the government regarded as "troublemakers." There were work stoppages and demonstrations. Many of the more strident demonstrators were threatened with violating the Espionage Act and were faced with $10,000 worth of fines and twenty-year prison terms. At Manzanar, an uprising occurred over the beating of a man who was an FBI informant. In the melee, a young Nisei was shot and killed, and nine others were wounded.

Fred Korematsu, Minoru Yasui, and Gordon Hirabayashi lost their cases before the US Supreme Court.

Legal Challenges

There were four legal challenges to the constitutionality of the internment that made their way to the Supreme Court. Mitsuye Endo, a government employee, filed a lawsuit of habeas corpus (a term for a court order allowing prisoners to be present to determine if they are being held legally). She was interned for more than two years before the Supreme Court ruled she was "entitled to unconditional release." By that time, the WRA had already begun returning some evacuees to the Pacific coast. Gordon Hirabayashi, a student at the University of Washington, defied the curfew and contended the curfew was racial discrimination restricting the rights of Japanese American citizens. Fred Korematsu was a US citizen who refused to be taken from his home. His case came to be known as *Korematsu v. United States*. Minoru Yasui, a law student in Oregon, tried many times to enlist but was turned away. When his father was evacuated, Yasui demanded to be arrested for defying the curfew. Yasui, Korematsu, and Hirabayashi lost their cases before the Supreme Court, which unanimously upheld the government's actions. Said Hirabayashi, "When my case was before the Supreme Court in 1943, I fully expected that as a citizen the Constitution would protect me. My citizenship didn't protect me one bit. Our Constitution was reduced to a scrap of paper."

FIVE

Looking for Closure

On September 8, 1943, General Dwight D. Eisenhower, commander in chief of the Allied Forces, announced, "The Italian Government has surrendered its armed forces unconditionally." On May 8, 1945, President Truman announced, "Nazi Germany has been defeated." He went on to say, "The Japanese people have felt the weight of our land, air, and naval attacks … The longer the war lasts, the greater will be the suffering and hardships which the people of Japan will undergo—all in vain. Our blows will not cease."

On July 26, 1945, President Truman, the president of China, and the prime minister of Great Britain issued what is known as the Potsdam Declaration, a call for Japan to surrender unconditionally. It asserted in part, "The full application of our military power, backed by our resolve, will mean the inevitable and complete destruction of the Japanese armed forces and just as inevitably the utter devastation of the Japanese homeland." Japan's military leaders, as well as the emperor's cabinet, remained divided. Soldiers believed

Opposite: **A Seattle family arrives home from the Minidoka internment camp to find their house has been vandalized.**

that surrender would dishonor those who fought and died. On August 6, 1945, a US bomber named the *Enola Gay* dropped the world's first atomic bomb on the industrial city of Hiroshima, Japan. Three days later, the United States dropped a second atomic bomb on the city of Nagasaki, and combined, more than 250,000 Japanese citizens died as a result of the bombs. Japan surrendered on August 14. The usually silent Emperor Hirohito proclaimed on September 2, 1945, the date of the formal surrender, "We command all our people forthwith to cease hostilities, to lay down their arms and faithfully to carry out all the provisions of the Instrument of Surrender."

Ex Parte Endo

As war with Japan raged, Mitsuye Endo, a twenty-two-year-old Japanese American clerical worker, was harassed by coworkers and then fired from her job with the California State Highway Commission. Soon she was detained and incarcerated at Tule Lake. The Japanese American Citizens League (JACL) was looking for a test case to file a writ of habeas corpus. They felt that because Endo was a citizen and a Christian, her brother was in the army, and neither had been to Japan or could read or speak Japanese, she would be a sympathetic plaintiff. Endo agreed.

JACL attorneys filed the habeas corpus petition and asked for Endo's release. They argued that her detention deprived her of the right to report to work and that the army had no right to detain a loyal American citizen who was innocent of the allegations used to justify her removal and incarceration.

Her case, known as *Ex Parte Endo*, was heard in July 1942, and not until July 1943 did the judge finally rule. He did so only by dismissing the case without explanation. JACL attorneys appealed to the Ninth Circuit Court of Appeals in April 1944, and this time, the judge deferred the case to the US Supreme Court. During the trials, Endo remained incarcerated. At one point, the War Relocation Authority offered her release if she would relocate somewhere other than the West Coast, thereby invalidating her lawsuit. Endo chose to remain in the internment camp. In October 1944, attorneys argued her case before the Supreme Court. The ruling was to come down on December 18, 1944. US government officials knew that the impending court decision would likely go in favor of Endo, thereby making the internment of loyal Japanese Americans unlawful. With that concern, the government quickly issued Public Proclamation Number 21 on December 17, 1944, which ended the mass imprisonment of Japanese American citizens as well as US residents with Japanese ancestry. President Roosevelt's suspicions about the verdict were correct, for on December 18, 1944, Justice William O. Douglas read the judges' unanimous decision on *Ex Parte Endo*, which said in part, "We are of the view that Mitsuye Endo should be given her liberty … For we conclude that, whatever power the War Relocation Authority may have to detain other classes of citizens, it has no authority to subject citizens who are concededly loyal." In a concurring opinion, Justice Frank Murphy wrote, "Detention in Relocation Centers of persons of Japanese ancestry … is another example of the unconstitutional resort to racism inherent in the entire evacuation program."

Beginning of the End

When the government issued Public Proclamation Number 21, titled "Persons of Japanese Ancestry Exemption from Exclusion Orders," Major General Henry Pratt announced that the release of the prisoners would begin January 2, 1945. For Japanese American internees, the proclamation gave them freedom, but for many, with the freedom came anger, confusion, bitterness, sadness, and loss. As the gates opened and the watchtowers were abandoned, many of the internees had no idea where they would go. For many, "going home" was not a clear path. As people departed the camps, the government gave them each just $25 and a train ticket.

Many internees saw their experience as an illegal imprisonment, while others believed internment was a permissible response to a wartime threat. Some people chose to try to regain what they had lost, while others chose to relocate farther east. Still others harbored such a deep resentment of their mistreatment that they moved to Japan. Some Issei had aged enough to feel they did not have the energy or the spirit to return to rebuild. As war with Japan continued, they were fearful. Some even wanted to stay in the camps, where they would be safe from attack from the whites in their old neighborhoods.

Stay Away!

As Japanese Americans left the camps, most discovered little was left of their homes, farms, businesses, property, and savings. Recalled former internee Aya Nakamura, "Finally getting out of the camps was a great day. It felt so good to get out of the gates, and just know that you were going home ... finally. Home wasn't where I left it though. Getting back, I was just shocked to see what had happened, our home being bought by a different family, different decorations in the windows; it was our house, but it wasn't anymore."

In many agricultural areas, white farmers resented the return of Japanese farmers. They resented the Japanese farmers' prowess and former success. Additionally, many whites had taken over Japanese farmland. Loggers, construction workers, dockworkers, factory workers, truck drivers, and other union tradespeople shared the farmers' viewpoint. They feared losing jobs to Japanese workers who had, in prior times, undermined union workers and

Seventy years after Marianne Rikimaru was sent to the Tule Lake internment camp, she was reunited with Beverly Pond and the antique dolls Pond kept in safekeeping.

accepted lower wages. Members of an organization called the Remember Pearl Harbor League (RPHL) were farmers and business people who protested the resettlement. The group published a pamphlet that in part read, "The Japanese were a menace until removed, and will become a menace again when returned. The Japs must not come back." A newspaper in a farming region south of Seattle ran a front-page headline, "OUR OBJECTIVE: BANISH JAPS FOREVER FROM THE USA," each day for several months. Seattle's *Post Intelligencer* ran an article by E. D. Phelan, an attorney who recommended that the RPHL "work for an amendment to the United States constitution which would revoke the American citizenship of all Japanese." The *Seattle Times* reported that the RPHL had a list of five hundred persons who had pledged not to sell, lease, or rent farms, homes, or stores to the returning evacuees.

As elsewhere, many internees returned to Oregon to find that their homes had been looted and their farms abandoned and overgrown. Even Japanese cemeteries had been vandalized. An American Legion war memorial in Hood River, Oregon, refused to include the names of sixteen Japanese American soldiers from Hood River who had fought in the war, including two who had died in defense of their country. Throughout the state, many white Oregonians called for deportation of the Japanese Americans who had once been their neighbors. Former governor Walter Pierce said, "We should never be satisfied until every last Jap has been run out and our constitution changed so they can never get back."

In California, most Japanese did not leave the camps immediately. Internee Fusa Tsumagari, a former resident of Los Angeles, wrote to a friend, "The news of being able to go back to California has been accepted with mingled feeling … Those with property are wanting to go back, but wondering how the sentiment will be." Farm buildings of the first family to return to California were dynamited.

Welcome Home

Although their experience was not typical, some internees were welcomed back to their communities. In some cases, such as in San Jose, California, the internees were welcomed by other racial minorities, and many Japanese Americans settled into ethnically diverse neighborhoods. Most returnees were completely impoverished. Starting over, many had to share housing or live in cheap boarding houses. Some became migrant workers or took whatever work they could find. But most Nisei and Sansei eventually found employment, had families, and became active in their communities. Some rebuilt within their former ethnic communities, such as in Little Tokyo in Los Angeles and Japantown in San Francisco.

In some communities, such as Bainbridge Island, Washington, or Fowler, California, in the Central Valley, white farmers cared for the Japanese farms and returned them when the internees were released. In Oregon, where internees were treated badly upon their return, animosity faded over time. Approximately 20 percent of the Nisei and Sansei did not return to the West Coast. Some moved east to New York or Boston. Others, grateful to the Midwest church groups that had opposed internment, chose to relocate to Indianapolis, Detroit, and other Midwest cities. The *Detroit Free Press* called the Japanese newcomers "loyal friends in the war against Japan."

Justice

California attorney general turned governor Earl Warren was a strident defender of the Japanese relocation policy. He held many racist views of the Japanese, which influenced his decisions. In 1943, when it appeared that the United States was gaining ground on the war with Japan, Warren resisted ending the internment, saying, "If the Japs are released no one will be able to tell a saboteur from any other Jap ... We don't want to have a second Pearl Harbor in California." Earl Warren went on to become the chief justice of the US Supreme Court, and ironically, he and justices Hugo Black and William O. Douglas consistently ruled in favor of civil rights, including the landmark ruling in *Brown v. Board of Education of Topeka*, which desegregated schools. All three of the justices had supported and ruled in favor of the internment, and none of them ever formally changed their mind. However, in his memoirs, Chief Justice Warren wrote, "I have since deeply regretted the removal order and my own testimony advocating it, because it was not in keeping with our American concept of freedom and the rights of citizens." He said further, "Whenever I thought of the innocent little children who were torn from home, school friends, and congenial surroundings, I was conscience-stricken. It was wrong to react so impulsively, without positive evidence of disloyalty."

Earl Warren was in favor of internment during his campaign for governor. Later, as the chief justice of the US Supreme Court, he regretted his stance.

Following the war, the government started showing misgivings as demand grew for an apology and reparation for Japanese Americans. In 1948, President Harry S. Truman signed the Japanese American Evacuation Claims Act and allocated reimbursement for some economic losses borne by Japanese Americans. In the next decade, the alien land laws were struck down and Congress granted the Issei the right to become US citizens. In 1976, President Gerald Ford officially rescinded Executive Order 9066, concluding with, "I call upon the American people to affirm with me this American Promise—that we have learned from the tragedy of that long-ago experience forever to treasure liberty and justice for each individual American, and resolve that this kind of action shall never again be repeated."

In the 1980s, attorneys filed a writ of coram nobis, (a legal action to overturn a ruling made in error). Attorneys argued that the government had held back information that would have refuted the "military necessity" of the internment. As a result, the Supreme Court convictions against Gordon Hirabayashi, Minoru Yasui, and Fred Korematsu were rescinded. After a decade of debate, Congress enacted the Civil Liberties Act in 1988 to formally apologize to Japanese Americans and award $20,000 to each survivor.

Nidoto Nai Yoni

Nidoto Nai Yoni means "Let it not happen again." The internment of Japanese Americans is regarded now as a shameful mistake on the part of the US government. In a desire to ensure it does not happen again, several memorials

The monument in the cemetery of the Manzanar Relocation Center bears the inscription, "Monument for the Pacification of Spirits."

have been erected to maintain public awareness. In 2000, the Japanese American Memorial to Patriotism During World War II was dedicated in Washington, DC, honoring Japanese American soldiers who served in World War II, as well as the Japanese Americans held in internment camps. The site of the Manzanar Relocation Center in California's Owens Valley is a national historic site, operated by the National Park Service. The Manzanar National Historic Site features barracks, mess halls, artifacts, exhibits, and Japanese gardens created by the internees. It was created to mark "the story of oppression, resistance, and the ability of a people to challenge the circumstances."

In 2015, the Topaz National Historic Site in Utah opened with a museum displaying artifacts, photographs, a library, and an art gallery that features the work of internees who

The Bainbridge Island Japanese American Exclusion Memorial honors those whose "homes, livelihoods, and culture were taken from them, yet they persevered."

attended a camp art school taught by interned University of California art professor Chiura Obata. The Minidoka National Historic Site in Idaho is another national historic site owned and operated by the National Park Service. Visitors walk an interpretive trail through the desert with outdoor exhibits explaining the culture, landscape, historic buildings, and daily camp life. Videos, books, and display panels inside the interpretive center tell the stories of individuals and their families.

An extension of the Minidoka National Historic Site is the Bainbridge Island Japanese American Exclusion Memorial located on the site of the dock where the Japanese Americans were forced onto ferries. The memorial features a 227-foot (69 m) long "story wall" that contains the names of the 227 residents who were evacuated. A ferry dock is held up by 150 posts representing the 150 citizens who returned to the island. An inscription on the memorial reads, "The word exclusion is so vital to completely tell this sad chapter of American history, because not only were one hundred twenty thousand Japanese Americans forcibly removed and placed behind barbed wire in American concentration camps, but anyone with a drop of blood of Japanese ancestry was forbidden to remain in the **exclusion zone**. We should remember and honor everyone who suffered from this unconstitutional violation of civil liberties, and vow to never let fear, hysteria, and prejudice deprive anyone of life, liberty and equal protection under the law."

Key Dates in the Japanese Internment

June 27, 1894: A US District Court rules that Japanese immigrants cannot become US citizens.

May 14, 1905: The Asiatic Exclusion League is formed.

December 7, 1941: Japanese military attacks Pearl Harbor.

December 8, 1941: United States declares war on Japan, entering World War II.

February 19, 1942: President Roosevelt signs Executive Order 9066, giving the military authority to evacuate anyone considered an enemy without a trial.

March 2, 1942: Lieutenant General John L. DeWitt creates exclusion zones—California, Oregon, Washington, and parts of Arizona.

March 18, 1942: The president establishes the War Relocation Authority (WRA).

March 21, 1942: The first groups of Japanese American community leaders arrive at the assembly center in Manzanar, California.

March 24, 1942: The first Civilian Exclusion Order is issued for Bainbridge Island, Washington. Two hundred twenty-seven Japanese Americans are given six days to prepare for evacuation.

March 28, 1942: Minoru Yasui turns himself in to a Portland police station for intentionally breaking curfew orders.

May 16, 1942: Gordon Hirabayashi refuses to register for relocation and turns himself in to the FBI. He is also charged with breaking the curfew on May 28.

May 29, 1942: American Friends Service Committee establishes the National Japanese American Student Relocation Council.

June 1, 1942: The WRA transforms Manzanar into the first internment camp.

August 10, 1942: The first inmates arrive at Minidoka, Idaho.

August 12, 1942: The first 292 inmates arrive at Heart Mountain, Wyoming.

August 27, 1942: The first inmates arrive at Granada, or Amache, Colorado.

September 11, 1942: The first inmates arrive at Topaz.

September 18, 1942: The first inmates arrive at Rohwer, Arkansas.

December 5, 1942: The "Manzanar Uprising" protests arrest of popular internees.

December 10, 1942: The WRA establishes an isolation prison at Moab, Utah.

February 1, 1943: The all-Japanese American 442nd Regiment is activated.

February 6, 1943: The WRA produces the Loyalty Questionnaire.

June 21, 1943: The Supreme Court delivers unanimous rulings in *Hirabayashi v. United States* and *Yasui v. United States*, upholding the government's actions. Hirabayashi is sent to federal prison.

September 13, 1943: Tule Lake becomes an isolation center for "No-No Boys" and other "troublemakers."

January 14, 1944: Nisei become eligible for the draft.

January 26, 1944: The Heart Mountain Fair Play Committee is organized.

October 27–30, 1944: The 442nd Regimental Combat Team rescues a Texas battalion that had been surrounded by German troops in France.

December 17, 1944: Public Proclamation Number 21 ends Japanese American internment.

December 18, 1944: The Supreme Court unanimously decides in favor of Mitsuye Endo.

January 2, 1945: Internees are allowed to return to the West Coast.

August 6 and 9, 1945: Atomic bombs are dropped on the Japanese cities of Hiroshima and Nagasaki.

August 14, 1945: Japan surrenders. The formal surrender ceremony is held on September 2.

March 20, 1946: Tule Lake releases the last of the internees.

July 2, 1948: President Truman signs the Japanese American Evacuation Claims Act, partially compensating Japanese Americans for economic loss.

June 27, 1952: Congress passes Immigration and Naturalization Act, granting Issei the right to become US citizens.

February 19, 1976: President Gerald Ford signs the proclamation formally terminating Executive Order 9066.

August 10, 1988: President Ronald Reagan signs the Civil Liberties Act, which grants $20,000 to each survivor of the internment camps.

assembly centers Quickly constructed facilities where internees were gathered before being assigned to permanent internment camps.

Bushido Japanese code of manners and moral and ethical conduct.

conscript To enlist persons compulsorily into military or labor service.

emigration The act of leaving one's country.

exclusion zone Area of military importance wherein "enemy aliens" were not allowed. Zones were located in Washington, Oregon, California, and parts of Arizona.

Executive Order 9066 Order issued authorizing the internment of all "enemy aliens," although most affected were Japanese Americans.

fifth column A term describing a group within one country that is sympathetic or working to aid the enemy.

habeas corpus petition A court order that commands a government official to bring a prisoner to court to determine whether the prisoner is being held legally.

immigrants People who move to another country.

internment Term used by the US government to express the detention and incarceration of Japanese Americans.

Issei First-generation Japanese residents of the United States.

Kibei Japanese American citizens educated in Japan.

Nippon Name by which Japanese call their country.

Nisei Second-generation Japanese Americans born as citizens of the United States.

relocation camp Euphemism for internment camp or concentration camp.

repatriation Return of someone to their own country.

sabotage The act of deliberately destroying, damaging, or obstructing an event, person, place, or thing.

Sansei Third-generation Japanese Americans, born as citizens of the United States.

Shinto An ancient Japanese religion.

shogun A Japanese feudal lord.

Books

Adams, Ansel. *Born Free and Equal: The Story of Loyal Japanese Americans.* Bishop, CA: Spotted Dog Press, 2002.

Gruenewald, Mary Matsuda. *Looking Like the Enemy: My Story of Imprisonment in Japanese-American Internment Camps.* Troutdale, OR: NewSage Press, 2005.

Lange, Dorothea. *Impounded: Dorothea Lange and the Censored Images of Japanese American Internment.* New York: Norton, 2006.

Shirai, Noboru. *Tule Lake: An Issei Memoir.* Sacramento, CA: Muteki Press, 2001.

Uchida, Yoshiko. *Desert Exile: The Uprooting of a Japanese-American Family.* Classics of Asian American Literature. Seattle, WA: University of Washington Press, 2015.

Media

Anderson, Cris, and John de Graaf. *Visible Target: On Nisei Internment.* Seattle, WA: KCTS Public Television, 1986.

The Cats of Mirikitani. New York: Arts Alliance America, 2008.

Discoveries ... America National Parks: Japanese American Incarceration 1942–1945. Issaquah, WA: Bennett Watt Productions, 2014.

Farewell to Manzanar. Adapted from Memoirs of Jeanne Wakatsuki Houston. Universal City, CA: NBC Universal Media, 2011.

Websites

Densho

http://www.densho.org

The Japanese American Legacy Project provides history of internment, an extensive encyclopedia, oral histories, and photo archives.

Japanese American National Museum

http://www.janm.org

This website promotes events and exhibitions about or by Japanese Americans and carries blog posts about the experience of the Japanese in the United States.

National Park Service

https://www.nps.gov/manz/index.htm
https://www.nps.gov/miin/index.htm

Websites of the Manzanar and Minidoka National Historic Sites detailing the history, present exhibits, and photo archives from these relocation centers.

PBS

http://www.pbs.org/childofcamp

Public Broadcasting Service's study of Japanese American internment, including history, documentaries, and further resources.

University of California Japanese American Relocation Digital Archives

http://www.calisphere.universityofcalifornia.edu/0/jarda

University of California's collection of the history of internment, primary sources, personal accounts, background of events, and daily life.

University of Washington Japanese American Exhibit and Access Project

http://www.lib.washington.edu/exhibits/harmony

University of Washington Japanese American and Canadian internment photo archives, articles, and oral histories.

Books

Inada, Lawson Fusao, ed. *Only What We Could Carry: The Japanese American Internment Experience.* Berkeley, CA: Heyday Books, 2000.

Neiwert, David. *Strawberry Days: How Internment Destroyed a Japanese American Community.* New York: Palgrave Macmillan, 2005.

Tunnell, Michael O., and George W. Chilcoat. *The Children of Topaz: The Story of a Japanese-American Internment Camp: Based on a Classroom Diary.* New York: Holiday House, 1996.

Uchida, Yoshiko. *The Invisible Thread: The Powerful Memoir of a Girl Consigned to a Concentration Camp—by the U.S. Government.* New York: Simon & Schuster, 1995.

Woodward, Mary. *In Defense of Our Neighbors. The Walt and Milly Woodward Story.* Bainbridge Island, WA: Fenwick, 2008.

Online Articles

"BIJAC History: Exclusion and Internment." Bainbridge Island Japanese American Community. Retrieved June 14, 2016. http://www.bijac.org/index.php?p=HISTORYExclusionInternment.

"Camp Harmony Exhibit." Japanese American Exhibit & Access Project, University of Washington. Retrieved June 14, 2016. http://www.lib.washington.edu/exhibits/harmony.

"Children of the Camps." Children of the Camps Project, Public Broadcasting Corporation. Retrieved June 14, 2016. http://www.pbs.org/childofcamp/resources/index.html.

Colasurdo, Luke. "The Internment of Japanese Americans as Reported by Seattle Area Weekly Newspapers." Seattle Civil Rights & Labor History Project, University of Washington, 2005. https://depts.washington.edu/civilr/news_colasurdo.htm.

Harper, Tim. "Japan's Giant Second World War Gamble." Guardian, September 7, 2009. http://www.theguardian.com/world/2009/sep/07/japan-imperialism-militarism.

"The Immigration Act of 1924 (The Johnson-Reed Act)." Milestones: 1921–1936, United States Department of State, Office of the Historian. Retrieved June 14, 2016. https://history.state.gov/milestones/1921-1936/immigration-act.

"Japanese Americans Interned During World War II." Telling Their Stories: Oral Histories Archives Project, Urban School of San Francisco. Retrieved June 14, 2016. http://www.tellingstories.org/internment.

"Japanese Life in Utah." Utah History to Go. Retrieved June 14, 2016. http://historytogo.utah.gov/people/ethnic_cultures/the_peoples_of_utah/japaneselifeinutah.html.

Mercier, Laurie. "Japanese Americans in the Columbia River Basin: Historical Overview." Columbia River Basin Ethnic History Archive, Washington State University, Vancouver. Retrieved June 14, 2016. http://archive.vancouver.wsu.edu/crbeha/ja/ja.htm.

"A More Perfect Union: Japanese Americans and the U.S. Constitution." Smithsonian National Museum of American History. Retrieved June 14, 2016. http://amhistory.si.edu/perfectunion/ non-flash/removal_main.html.

"Most of Japs' Lands Shifted." *San Francisco News*, April 21, 1942. http://www.sfmuseum.org/hist8/land1.html.

"New Order on Aliens Awaited." *San Francisco News*, March 2, 1942. http://www.sfmuseum.org/hist8/evac16.html.

"Preserving California Japantowns." California Japantowns. Retrieved June 14, 2016. http://www.californiajapantowns.org/ profiles.html.

Takei, Barbara. "Tule Lake." Densho Encyclopedia. Retrieved June 14, 2016. http://encyclopedia.densho.org/Tule%20Lake.

INDEX

Page numbers in **boldface** are illustrations. Entries in **boldface** are glossary terms.

Adams, Ansel, 93, 95
Asiatic Exclusion League, 21, 31–33, 47–48
assembly centers, 73–76, 82

Bainbridge Island, 20, 63, 74, 91–92, 107, 112–113, **112**
Bushido, 30

conscript, 13, 16, 18

DeWitt, John, 62–65, 68–69, **69**, 94

emigration, 10, 13–14, 46, 86
Endo, Mitsuye, 99, 102–103
exclusion zone, 113
Executive Order 9066, 70–71, 73, 90–91, 94, 96–97, 110

fifth column, 64
442nd Regiment, 85

habeas corpus petition, 94, 99, 102
Hirabayashi, Gordon, 99, **99**, 110

immigrants, 9, **14**, 15–16, 18–23, 26, 33, 44–46, **46**, 51–52, 54–55, 57–58, 61
Inouye, Daniel, 71, 84–85
internment
   aftermath of, **101**, 104–108, **105**, 110–113
   daily life during, 74–80
   end of, 102–194
   evacuation process, **63**, 71–75, 91–92
   legal authorization, 68–71
   opposition to, 7, 78, 80–81, 83–84, 89–99, 102–103
   outside the US, 85–87
   statistics, 6, 74, 82–83
Issei, 20–22, 24–25, 27, 30–31, 49, 52, 55, 76, 80, 83–84, 94, 97, 104, 110

Japanese Americans
   assimilation, 26–27, 30–31

126 **Internment: Japanese Americans in World War II**

ABOUT THE AUTHOR

Ruth Bjorklund lives on Bainbridge Island, Washington. Author of numerous books, she has a master's degree in library and information science from the University of Washington. The Japanese Americans in her hometown were the first to be evacuated. On the site of an old ferry dock stands the Bainbridge Island Japanese American Exclusion Memorial where evacuees began their journey to the internment camps.